THE FLIPPING
BLUEPRINT

*The Complete Plan for Flipping Houses and
Creating Your Real Estate–Investing Business*

LUKE WEBER

CONTENTS

Acknowledgments

Special thanks to my wife Yvette and my son
Ashur, you are my why.

Tony P for helping make this happen.

To my parents for teaching me values, respect and
how to share.

Finally, to all of my business associates, friends
and my ever expanding network. We all
succeed together.

Introduction –

Who Am I and Why a Blueprint?

The year was 2001 when I quit my job. I was managing a travel company for a boss who was the definition of awful. He had just gone off on a particularly nasty, expletive-filled, and sexist tirade in front of multiple employees, stormed out of my office, and slammed his door like a child. I had had enough. I packed up my belongings, walked into his office and dropped my keys on his desk, and told him "I'm out." He looked up at me and said, "Do you know what this does to me? I should shoot you right now." He kept a loaded gun in his desk. I calmly turned around and walked out of his office, gathered up my belongings, and left. I was done, I was free. For the next few months I traveled and enjoyed the stress-free life of being unemployed. However, my finances, or lack thereof, soon caught up with me. With my savings dwindling, my checking account decided it was time for me to get a new job. After the high stress levels and long hours of my last job, I wanted something simple, something stress-free, something easy. I looked through the want ads and answered a data-entry position at an appraisal company, and that is where my real estate journey began.

I quickly went from the data-entry position to getting my appraiser's license. After a year of learning how to evaluate residential properties, I took the plunge when I was 22 years old and bought my first property. A $134,000 two-bedroom/two-bathroom condominium located in Las Vegas. The condo had been a rental property for an out-of-state investor and looked the part. I doubted the tenant had ever cleaned. Dust was piled on top of every surface it could cling to, footpaths were carved into the carpet, and the smell would have been enough to turn away your standard buyer. Thankfully I wasn't standard. I negotiated the price down from $145,000 with a few thousand dollars in seller-paid closing costs thrown in and bought the property with a Federal Housing Administration (FHA) loan. I found contractors to carpet and paint the property. I found other contractors to lay tile and install granite countertops. I bought materials and installed fixtures and completed small repairs myself. You quickly learn the extent and limits of your construction skills when an electrical current is coursing through your body. I moved into the property before the work was done and continued to work on it evenings and weekends. I overpaid contractors, the project took twice as long as it should have, and I overimproved the property. I did almost everything wrong, but when it was time to sell I sold the property for $279,500 and made more than $80,000! I was hooked. I bought another property, then two more; I moved from one house to another. I started buying rentals and making passive money. 2004 and 2005 rolled through and it was hard to not make money on real estate. Everyone could qualify for a loan, and you could buy a house and sell it the next day for a profit. But it couldn't, it wouldn't, last. The final property I bought before it all came tumbling down was on June 30, 2005, a dream home for my wife and me. I had my own appraisal company I was running out of my home office, and the real estate investing was just a side gig at that time. A way for us to take nice vacations and buy a bigger and better home. But I saw the market shifting, red flags began popping up. I saw new-home builders start offering more incentives to buyers. I saw inventory levels of houses increasing. I became nervous and cancelled the contracts that I had on several new-construction properties. Although the real estate industry was passionately telling people to keep buying houses, it was looking like this fun roller-coaster ride we had all been on was about to take a plunge. I tried to warn my friends, but the hype kept pushing people to buy well past the point of no return. I began selling my properties in 2006, but we had already reached the pinnacle and were headed down faster than I could have imagined. The pace quickened, and we began screaming our way to the bottom through 2007 to 2009 as the Las Vegas market dropped 65% from its peak values. Business came to a halt, and my family, like many others across the country, felt the collapse of an inflated economy. If you didn't know it already, I hope you do now, real estate markets are full of up and downs.

After years of struggling and fighting our way through issue after issue, reduced work, financial stress, dwindling accounts, I finally saw a change in the market. It was 2010 and it was time to buy. But not like before. The speculative purchases people were making from 2003 to 2007 were gone. I began to do more research and became a more knowledgeable buyer. My wife and I cashed out the $80,000 that we had left in the stock market and went all in. We began to flip. But not like before; we were not going to get hurt like that again. We began to buy rentals again. But not like before. Things started to look up for us. We started making profits again. I bought a new home for my family, a short sale that was a steal, because the banks didn't know how to handle their inventory. Then one night in January 2012 everything changed. It was that time in the evening when you check your phone before going to bed, there shouldn't be any calls, everything is fine, and you can go to sleep. I had three missed calls and three voice mails. I listened to the voice mails and heard a distressed voice come through the phone speaker, muffled by the sound of sirens. My father had had a heart attack. My father, my friend, my son's Opa. I raced to the hospital, 80 miles an hour down 35-mile-an-hour roads. I still vividly remember that nighttime drive, me repeating to myself "No, no, no" all the way to the hospital. When I arrived I had to run from one side of the hospital to the other, three different desks I had to stop at to find him. Frantic, I remember the looks on the nurses' faces; they already knew. No matter how fast I went, it was already too late. He was gone, just like that. I was hit, I was knocked down. It sometimes takes a shock for you to figure out your life and whether you are on the path you want to be on. It took me 6 months to fight through my depression, my pain, to realize I wasn't doing what I wanted and I wasn't providing for my family the way I wanted. I was working too hard and not getting anywhere. Time is precious, time with your family is precious. I was working 10- to 12-hour days, 6 and 7 days a week. I had to change what I was doing. Again I doubled down on real estate, as I knew this was the path to recovering my time and reaching financial freedom. At this point I was flipping a house about every 2 months, but still as a side gig, I knew there had to be a better approach. There had to be ways to be more efficient, more profitable. I closed the doors of my appraisal business and I began going to real estate–investing seminars, paying tens of thousands of dollars sometimes. I would pick up a little bit of knowledge here and there. If I only learned one thing, gathered one missing piece of information at each of these events that would save me or make me $1,000 on a deal, and I could repeat that experience 100 times, the seminars would more than pay for themselves.

Sitting in one of these rooms, I finally took stock of who was there with me. It was a $40,000 event and there were about 500 people in the room. Most of them didn't know a thing about real estate, and I had to wonder how many of these people could have even afforded to be there. Over the course of that weekend I found out that many of these people had maxed out credit cards, had borrowed money from family, or had taken out a second mortgage to attend. I was frustrated. I was sad. Most of these people had drunk the Kool-Aid and were starstruck by these pseudo-celebrities and were being taught next to nothing! I was there to hopefully find one or two nuggets of gold; these people were there because they thought they were going to get the keys to the kingdom! The guru at this particular event answered one of my questions while he was on stage by telling me to just use Google to find my answer! In this room of 500 people who each paid $40,000, he was telling me, and all of them, the answers were on Google. So why did I, why did we all pay him $40,000? Well, guess what, it was on Google, not all the information I was looking for, but parts of it. There were still missing pieces to the answer of my question, to everyone's questions. Pieces these gurus didn't know or couldn't provide. I had other attendees coming up to me at these seminars addressing questions to me instead of to the staff who were the supposed "experts." Little did we know that these staff members who were paraded around as the "experts" had for the most part never even flipped a house! They were just salespeople trying to gain your trust for the next upsell. Maybe you have also paid $20,000, $50,000, even $80,000 to attend a real estate–investing course and learn what a guru said was the best way to "flip a house" using his or her secret formula that could make you rich just like him or her. You went to the classes, the boot camps, the bus tours, the action-packed weekends with lots of jumping and dancing and "getting out of your comfort zone," but you still can't get a realtor to work with you or find you flippable properties. Your education materials are sitting on a shelf or in a closet just collecting dust. Why isn't this working? You are not alone. There are tens of thousands of people who have gone to these seminars and have not been able to achieve anything with the limited education they received. Did you ever stop to think and ask the guru when he or she actually worked on projects? Probably not. Most gurus are no longer making money in real estate (a lot never even did!). You paid big money to be taught outdated, watered-down, and generic principles that don't work. These gurus are making their money (millions of dollars) selling their education systems and are so far detached from the real estate world that most couldn't even do what is being taught in their programs.

There are too many *missing pieces* in what they teach. What they were teaching was the equivalent of a blueprint for a house with no doors, windows, electrical, or plumbing. They would tell you about the floor, the walls, and the roof and just ignore all of the other missing pieces. But I needed more, the other attendees needed more (and paid for more). Even if you have never attended a real estate–investing seminar, you can understand my frustration. People were being taken advantage of, money was coerced out of their pockets, and they were given next to nothing in return. I learned what I could from the seminars. I found other active investors and learned what they were doing. I built and grew my real estate business one flip at a time, one rental at a time. I took the education that I earned, learned, paid for and created over the past 15 years and now have made it into a thriving business.

So why should you keep reading? Just because I know how to use Google? Since 2001 I have been part of thousands of transactions across the country, I have flipped hundreds of properties (everything from manufactured homes to apartment buildings), I have owned and sold rental portfolios, I have raised millions of dollars of private funds, and I *am still active in this business*! That's right. I have been very successful, and I am going to teach you from the ground up what I wish I had known from day one. The teaching that I and many others paid tens of thousands of dollars for at these seminars, but didn't receive. It doesn't matter if you are just starting out or have been in this business for years, there are missing pieces in your education, and I want to give you those pieces. I want you to have the entire blueprint. I want you to learn from my trials, my mistakes, my successes, and all of the tips and tricks I have learned and created during my 15-year journey in this business. There is no reason for you to drink the Kool-Aid and go $50,000 or $100,000 into debt to pay for pieces of this education like so many people do. This is why I wrote this book and created this blueprint for you to flip a house and create your own real estate–investing business.

This book contains my business. The step-by-step processes, the ideas and methods that I use in my business day in and day out to connect with real estate professionals, find deals, raise money, locate and manage contractors, and maximize profits on my flips. I have poured my knowledge and experiences into the following pages so that you can be successful. I truly believe anyone can succeed in this business. However, this is not a get-rich-quick scheme, this is not a smoke-and-mirrors show, this is the real deal. I know the stresses and struggles of getting a real estate–investing business started, and I want to fast track you. Whether you only want to do one or two flips a year to fund your retirement or you want to create a full-time business running 100 flips a year, the tools, tricks, and methods within this book will help you get to where you want to be. If you put in the work, you will reap the rewards! I now have the time to spend with my family, the time to coach my son's soccer team while other fathers sadly can't make it to practice or even a game, the time to take my wife out on day dates, the time to travel the world with my family. I do all of this while I still flip houses. I don't say this to brag, I say this to let you know it is possible for you as well. Whether you like fancy cars, expensive shoes, or travel, this business can be the key for you to reclaim your time and reach financial freedom! Throughout this book you will come across suggestions and think "I should do that." Whenever you have one of those thoughts, I want you to mark your page, put your book down, and put the idea you just read into action. Your success is dependent upon you acting upon these suggestions. It is always easy to say "I will do it later or tomorrow," but if you want to get your business moving, you need to do things now! There are also call-to-action items throughout this book—places where I will tell you to do an activity or a task. Stop your reading and do the activity. I want you to be successful, and everything within this book is something I have done in the past, something I believe in, and something that I currently do, and together these ideas I am sharing will help you reach the level of success you desire.

CHAPTER 1 –

Who are you? Creating your "Real Estate Story"

Before we get started, we need to do something very important. We need to figure out who you are and what your story is. Why do we need to do this? Because a story you believe is a story you can sell. Your story is the foundation of this whole blueprint. We all come from different walks of life. I wasn't born into a wealthy family. I do not have a college education. I am not perfect. But I do know my story, and with that, I can communicate who I am and what I need to the people I encounter in my business life. Whether it be a realtor, a wealthy individual looking to invest with me, or a contractor I need to complete a project. Every day I meet new people who don't know me, and it is my story that convinces them to do business with me. If you can communicate who you are and what you need, they typically will want to work with you. How do you find out who you are? Chances are most of you do not consider yourselves real estate investors yet. You may feel like a newbie. You may question why people would want to work with you. The fact is, you are already a real estate investor, no matter what your experience has been to this point. You already have a real estate story, you just have to find it. Let me give you a few examples of how I have helped students develop their real estate stories:

Joan. I once had a student who had just been let go from her job. Was she unemployed? No. She was newly retired and had extra time on her hands to devote to this new career in real estate. Retired? Wow! That must mean she was successful at her job and has money to spend, thinks the realtor. Weakness to strength. Now Joan didn't actually have much money, certainly not enough to buy a house for cash, so how did we tackle that? Joan let the realtors she was talking with know that her friends, who were still working, had plenty of money but no time and wanted to invest with her—she was the face for their group. Did Joan have these friends yet? No, but she knew where to find them, and she knew she would (we'll talk about the power of networking in chapter 11). Retired versus unemployed. The words you use shape people's perception of you. Were these lies? No. Was it a story the student was able to believe and then to sell? Yes.

Rich. Another student of mine had moved to Nevada for a better paying job, but his wife and children stayed behind in California so his kids could continue in their local school. Rich found a property to rent in Nevada and would visit his family in California on the weekends. He and his wife had bought a couple of houses over the years and sold them, just your standard moving up to a bigger house as their family grew. But does it have to be a standard story? No. He began to introduce himself as a real estate investor from California who had been buying and selling property there for the last 20 years; he had started investing in rental property in Nevada and was looking to expand his business. Most realtors love out-of-state investors, as they typically associate those investors with having money. Were these lies? No. Find your story, there is always something beyond standard; you just have to find it.

Miguel. Miguel's father was an unsuccessful real estate developer in California and had lost a lot money over his lifetime, but Miguel, my student, saw what could have happened if his father had made better choices. This gave Miguel his passion to get into real estate. Miguel's story became that his father was a pioneer in Los Angeles real estate development in the 1960s and 1970s, and Miguel wanted to go out on his own and apply what his father had taught him. People want to work with successful people. I am sure you have all heard the saying "fake it till you make it." But you don't even have to fake it! You have a story, you just have to find it!

Take a few minutes and write down what your real estate experiences have been to this point in your life.

- How many houses have you lived in?

- How many houses have you bought or sold?

- How many houses have you rented?

- Have you ever owned a rental property (even if you just rented out a room to a cousin for a summer)?

- If you have ever bought a new-construction home you can let people know that you have done ground-up construction.

- If you have money in the stock market (even if it is only $1,000), you can tell people you want to transition your money out of the stock market and put it into real estate.

- Did your parents ever buy a house and sell it? Guess what, that is a flip! There is no definitive time frame in which a flip has to be completed.

You might be asking yourself at this point: "What if they ask me for specifics?." They typically don't. Questions will typically be generic in nature, just a polite conversation. Keep your answers short and sweet and bring the conversation back to what you are doing and needing now. Real estate professionals are so engrossed in the now and how you can make them money that they typically won't ask for in-depth details about your past. Their response after they hear your real estate story is typically, "Wow that's great, so how can I help you? What do you need from me?." Once you have your real estate story, it becomes so much easier to talk to these realtors, private investors, and contractors. If you believe in yourself and your story, they will believe too. You also need to understand most of the real estate professionals you encounter will know less about real estate investing than you after you read this book. They may act like they have experience, they may try to make you believe they are experts, but most likely their experiences are limited and incomplete. You will find yourself quickly becoming their teacher.

You have your story. What's next? The following chapters will show you how to pick the market you want to be in, how to find the deals and make offers, how to find funding and finance your deals, and how to then remodel and sell your properties. These pointers are all taken straight from my day-to-day business. This is what I do. Why am I sharing all of this with you? Am I worried the market will get saturated with new investors who will gobble up all the good deals and leave nothing for me? No. There are plenty of deals out there for you, for me, for everyone. The secret is that properties are always getting older and always needing to be remodeled, families are always growing or getting smaller, people get hired and fired every day, people get tired of living in the heat, people get tired of living in the cold. There are always reasons why a house has to be sold, and there is a never-ending supply of inventory, so let me show you how to find it!

CHAPTER 1 FLIP TIPS

1. Why do you need a story?

2. What do the other guys teach?

3. Three examples: the "retiree," the renter, and the son.

4. Truth is what sells your story.

5. We all have real estate experience. Do you live in a house or rental? You are already an experienced real estate investor!

6. After reading this book, you will have more knowledge than 98% of the real estate professionals you meet.

CHAPTER 2 –

How to Analyze Markets Like the Experts

Most gurus and real estate education companies don't do the research for you and say "Go invest in Alpine, Wyoming. It's the number one place for you to make money in redeveloping real estate!" Heck, most real estate education companies don't even provide you with the simple tools that those of us who are active and successful in this business use to decide which markets to invest in. A typical response you might hear at a seminar is "Go invest where other people are showing success. If they can do it, so can you!" Wouldn't it be better if they told you *why* those other people chose that market? This is how to research and choose your market the way successful investors do it:

Market choice: Start with the market that is closest to you and has a population of more than 100,000 (I personally prefer markets with more than 1,000,000 people; the bigger the market, the more opportunity there will be). This is your "local market." Or if you just don't want to work in that market, pick one that you have some type of emotional or sentimental attachment to. We call this *remote investing*. (Just a note, it is always easier to invest locally. If you do remote investing, I recommend going after higher profit margins for safety. I typically require an extra 25% on my bottom line for what I need to make; i.e., a $40,000 minimum profit line adjusts to $50,000.) Maybe you grew up there. Maybe it's where your spouse's family lives. Maybe it's just the location of your favorite professional sports team. No matter which of these reasons you use to choose your remote market, having an emotional attachment and, hopefully, a little background on the actual city will give you a greater desire to work there and keep grinding, as there is a lot of work involved in getting your flipping machine set up. Take note, though, this is the last time we are going to talk about making an emotional decision, as emotion has no place in your deal decisions, which should only be based on numbers and facts. If you can't decide whether you are making an emotional decision, put the numbers in front of someone else and get his or her opinion based on the numbers. If emotions are skewing your judgment, you are putting yourself at risk.

Also, don't spread yourself too thin. I have had students tell me they are working in five or six cities but can't find any deals. They are spread too thin and can't commit their resources appropriately. Start with one or at most two markets and then find the following items for your selected market:

Housing inventory levels: You want to find out how many homes are actually listed for sale in your selected market. If inventory levels are low, that is good. Some people view this as being bad, because "it's too hard to get deals here." Every market I work in I hear the same responses from realtors and other investors:

"You're too late, all the deals are gone."

"You should have been here two years ago."

"The big players are getting all the deals, you won't find anything."

If I hear these kinds of responses, it usually means I am in the right place but talking to the wrong person. You want to find people who, even though they might say these things, can follow it up with a positive statement. Such as:

"… but I found a good deal last month for another investor."

"… but there are still deals out there."

"… If they are finding them, I'm sure I can find you one too."

It might be challenging at first, but once you get that deal, if it is priced appropriately, you are most likely going to have a quick resale, as there will be little competition when your house has been rehabbed and placed back on the market. I complete my projects in markets that have little inventory or are classified as "seller's markets."

Selecting a realtor: Once you have your market nailed down, it's time to start contacting realtors. Why use a realtor? Licensed realtors, also referred to as real estate agents or agents, will have access to their local multiple listing service, or MLS for short. The MLS is an online data source that realtors use to list real estate available for rent or sale along with historical data on prior rentals and sales. The MLS is the best resource for residential real estate, better than any other website out there. To gain access to the MLS, you have to be a licensed individual (typically a realtor or appraiser), pay dues, sign a code of conduct, and so on. There is private and personal data throughout the MLS system that is not available to the general public. That is why you need realtors working with you. Additionally, MLS systems are city or region specific. If you have a realtor in Tampa, Florida, he or she won't be able to access the MLS for Boise, Idaho. So how do I decide which realtors to contact? I have been most successful accessing Zillow.com. Go there and click the Agent Finder button on the top toolbar. Next, enter your chosen market into the Location field. This will typically bring up twenty-five pages of agents. Do not go to the realtors listed as "featured" agents found on the top toolbar or even the realtors on the first three pages! If a realtor is listed as a featured agent or shows up on the first few pages of any website, he or she is not typically the best realtor for investors, just the realtor who paid the most for marketing! These realtors would rather deal with people looking to immediately buy or sell a home and aren't hungry enough to deal with a new investor like you. Solution? Go to page 25 and work your way back. You also want to avoid realtors who have more than one person in the photo or have the words "team" or "group" in their listings. You want to know who you are dealing with directly, as the personal level is what you are after. You want realtors who are hungry, motivated, and want to work with new clients. So should you pick up the phone and call them? Nope. That is a cold call and an ineffective use of your time. Send an email message through Zillow instead. In the time it would take to make one phone call, you can email ten or twenty realtors! What should you write or ask? Send the email I send: "I do residential redevelopment and I want to expand my business into the XYZ city area. If you work with investors, I'd love to ask you a couple quick questions that shouldn't take more than a few minutes of your time. If you can help me with this, please call or email me back." This way they can call or email you if they are interested in working with you. (HINT: Email is the preferred method for successful real estate investors, as it is a more efficient use of your time than speaking on the phone.) Now you are no longer making cold calls, and realtors are contacting you for your business! When they contact you, you will probably have to go through the introduction chit-chat with them. Let them talk, give brief answers to their questions, and stay on the topic of what you need from them. To find out the housing inventory levels, here are the three questions you need to ask:

1. How many single-family home *active* listings are there in your entire MLS currently?

2. How many single-family homes sold in the last 30 days in your entire MLS?

3. What is the average days on market (DOM) of those single-family homes sold in the past 30 days in the entire MLS?

If I have them on the phone, I will go over the three questions and ask if they can supply that information. They may ask you to repeat the questions or tell you they will send you their local market reports. These market reports are generic market stat reports from the MLS that are typically created every month and don't give you the most current snapshot. Let them know that you will email them the questions along with your contact information and that if they can just respond to the questions you are asking it would be appreciated. Keep it as easy as possible for them, and they are more likely to do it.

I send this message out to as many realtors as it takes to get at least three to respond and send me the numbers. (NOTE: It is important to stress only single-family homes and the entire MLS when asking the three questions.) This task should take a competent realtor between 5 and 10 minutes to answer all three questions. Ask them to email you the three separate numbers. You don't want them to send you all of the individual listings. The reply should look something like this:

Here are the numbers you requested—

7,250 active listings in the MLS;

2,600 sales in the past 30 days; and

53 average days on market.

That's it. Nothing fancy and no attachments necessary. You just want these three simple numbers. Once you get these numbers from at least three realtors, what do you do with them? First, check them against one another for accuracy. If the three sets of numbers are drastically different, you may need to call the realtors and find out what they actually searched. Once you have established that the numbers are accurate, divide the number of active listings by the number of sales. For example, if a realtor tells you there are 7,250 active listings and there were 2,600 sales of single-family homes in the past 30 days, here is the equation:

$$7,250/2,600 = 2.78$$

The 2.78 figure is the amount of months of available inventory; this is called an *absorption study*. If no additional properties were listed, it would take 2.78 months for the current number of available homes to be bought. So how do you use these numbers to determine whether you should be in this particular market?

Less than 4 months: A market with less than 4 months of inventory is a hot market, or undersupplied. You want to be in these markets. There is less competition for your home when you go to sell it, so it should sell for top price and quickly. This would be considered a *seller's market*. A seller's market is one that is favorable to a home seller, not a home buyer. NOTE: If there is less than 1 month of available inventory, that is considered a hypermarket, and competition is fierce! Properties in a hypermarket typically get multiple offers and sell above list price.

4–6 months: A market with 4–6 months of inventory is a *stable market*. Be cautious in these markets, as properties will typically take longer to sell and will not garner top prices because potential home buyers have more choices.

6 months or more: Stay out of a market with more than 6 months of inventory. There is too much competition, and this would be considered a *buyer's market*. A buyer's market is one that is favorable to a home buyer, not a home seller. Homes in buyer's markets typically have longer times on the market and sell for less than their asking prices.

Besides the amount of available inventory, you also want to check how many days the average property is listed for before it receives a contract. This is referred to as the days on market, or DOM for short. Your realtors will get this number when they do the search for the single-family homes sold in the past 30 days. So what does this number mean?

60 days or fewer: This is your ideal market. With an average DOM of 60 or fewer, your remodeled and ready to move in home will typically get a purchase contract in less than 30 days, and possibly multiple offers, since your house will be nicer and more desirable and will therefore sell faster than the average home. Buyers in these markets want a home and they want it now! This time frame is typically found in a hot market, a seller's market.

60–90 days: This is a slower market, maybe due to a seasonal shift or an increase in supply or buyers feeling less optimistic about the economy and their financial situations, which means they aren't chomping at the bit to make a large purchase like a home. Be cautious about entering a market in this range. This time frame is typically found in a stable market, but it could quickly turn into a buyer's market.

91+ days: Stay out of these markets! Holding costs add up and prices go down. This time frame is typically found in a buyer's market. The buyer gets to call the shots, not you, the seller.

Remember to get these numbers from at least three different realtors. They will typically be slightly different; however, they should still fall into a tight range. Just like any numbers someone provides you, they can be skewed one way or the other. Not only are you double-checking if your market is a good one to be in, you are triple-checking. That is how important it is to do your research on where you are investing. Once I have picked my market or markets, I continue to run these numbers once every month. This way I can react to any changes in the market quickly and efficiently.

So you've picked your market or at most two markets you wai to enter, you ran your numbers to make sure your chosen market is a hot market or a seller's market, and now it's time to understand how to analyze a deal and get properties to come to you!

CHAPTER 2 FLIP TIPS

1. Local versus remote—find somewhere you have a connection.

2. Size of market should be 100,000 plus, preferably 1 million plus—think Los Angeles, California, not Bloomington, Illinois.

3. Inventory levels—less than 4 months preferred, never more than 6 months.

4. Days on market (DOM)—less than 60 days, never more than 90.

5. Double-check and then triple-check!

6. Choose one or two markets at most, don't overextend yourself.

7. Keep your finger on the pulse of the market, run your market stats every month.

CHAPTER 3 –

The "No Formula" Formula: How to
Run Your Numbers and Accurately
Determine After-Repair Value (ARV)

Real estate investing is one of the most lucrative ways to make money in our modern age. Every day it seems there is another TV show with someone flipping a house. Every day there is another news article about how much money you can make investing in real estate. Every day there is another program teaching you how to invest in real estate by flipping houses, buying at auctions, investing in tax liens, investing in notes, buying cash-flow properties—an endless stream of real estate–investing that could possibly make you money.

But what most of these programs don't show you is how to find the single most important number in real estate investing, the *after-repair value*, commonly referred to as the ARV. Sure, some of them may have their methods, but how accurate are they really?

First, let's ask, "What *is* an ARV?" An after repair value, the ARV, is what your property will be worth after you have improved it. That means it is the most probable selling price of your property. Seems like a pretty important number when you are flipping a home, right? However, it's important for other kinds of real estate investing as well. For instance, if you are buying a property to become a long-term rental, wouldn't it be good to know what it will refinance for once you have it improved and it is performing with a renter in place? If you are investing in notes, you still need to know the value of a property. Even when I purchase an apartment building, I will focus on this value, so I know what the resale value is. If you want to make money in real estate, the ARV is the single most important number of *any* real estate transaction and is a number you should have before you make an offer. If you don't know how much you can sell a house for, how do you know how much you should pay for it? In real estate investing, we make our money when we buy the property and we collect it when we sell. If you don't buy it at the right price, there won't be any money to collect when you sell it.

Before we get into the "how," let's discuss the "why." Why is the ARV of a project considered the most important number in any real estate transaction? You may think the purchase price or the cost of repairs is important, and both are, but if you don't know what you can actually sell the property for (or refinance it for), then you don't know how much to pay for the property or the extent of the repairs you should undertake. Some people may argue the repair number is the most important number of a real estate transaction. If you are 10% off on your repair budget, is that going to kill your deal?

$2,000 tacked onto a $20,000 repair budget?

$5,000 tacked onto a $50,000 repair budget?

$10,000 tacked onto a $100,000 repair budget?

Are these numbers that are going to kill your deals? They shouldn't be deal killers. (If they are, you need to increase your profit margins, as that is way too narrow a profit line and is considered a risky transaction.) Now let's look at your ARV. If you are 10% off on an ARV, is that going to kill your deal?

$180,000 instead of $200,000 = $20,000 difference

$360,000 instead of $400,000 = $40,000 difference

$900,000 instead of $1,000,000 = $100,000 difference

In these three scenarios, the difference is most likely the majority of your profit and possibly even a loss. I do not buy real estate to *lose* money. I do not buy real estate to *hopefully* make money. I do not buy real estate to *maybe* make money. What I (and you) do can be summed up in a simple but very accurate statement: I buy real estate to make money. Definitive. Precise. Simple. But if you are not saying it with the same conviction I do, you may find yourself uttering one of the three prior statements. So how can I say, "I buy real estate to make money" with such conviction? Because I know how to accurately determine my ARV. There is no speculation, no gambling, no hoping, and no praying.

So why should you listen to me and not someone else? I am sure there are some other people out there saying what I am saying or something similar, but I can tell you that most are not. Every week I see someone giving free advice or selling another program about how to get rich quick in real estate or how to build long-term wealth or how to wholesale real estate without ever using any of your own money. Most of these programs teach one of these methods to determine ARV:

1. Ask your realtor what the ARV is.

2. Ask three realtors what the ARV is.

3. Take an average price of recently sold properties.

4. Take an average price per foot of the recently sold properties.

5. Find the highest sale in the neighborhood and use that.

6. Use a Zillow estimated value.

7. Order an appraisal.

8. Ask the homeowner what the property is worth.

Really? Let's go through these and see why they do not work.

1. **Ask your realtor what the ARV is.** Your realtor is
    your expert, right? He or she found you the property and
    may have even flipped a house in the past. He or she is a
    trained and licensed individual and has to operate with
    your best interests in mind. Right? Some are and some do,
    yes. But not most. Most realtors, when they send you a
    property to make an offer on, have already calculated their
    commission. What!? Realtors are concerned about getting
    paid? Of course they are. And for you realtors reading
    this and thinking that I am bashing realtors, I am not, it's
    just the truth, so don't tune me out or what I have to say.
    Realtors are definitely an important resource in your real
    estate–investing career and you need them. However, keep
    in mind that they are getting paid when you buy and sell
    a house. Their pay is not based on whether you make a
    profit or not. Every week I have realtors bring me new deals
    across the country, and so many of them have absolutely
    no support to their ARVs. In fact, if you ask most realtors
    for an ARV, they will look at you blankly. They typically
    don't even know what ARV means! Most will just say they
    "really know the area" or they can "sell it all day long for
    $400,000." Yet when they send you comparable sales, the
    highest sale is only $325,000 and is 500 square feet larger,
    has an extra bedroom and bathroom, and has a toilet made
    out of pure 24-karat gold! We do not invest based on feel-
    ings, especially the feelings and beliefs of others. You have
    to train realtors to give you what you want. If a realtor is

giving you an ARV, he or she better be giving you the proof of the ARV as well (don't worry, we'll get to that).

2. **Ask three realtors what the ARV is.** Out of the eight items I listed above, this is going to be the most accurate method, as you are getting three different opinions, and only one of those realtors will be getting paid on the purchase of the property. However, all three are still going to be concerned with getting the listing so they can get paid when you go to sell the property. Typically, you will get three different answers on the ARV from three different realtors, as their ARVs are just opinions. For instance, Realtor 1 may tell you the ARV is $350,000; Realtor 2 may say $400,000; and Realtor 3 may say $420,000. What do you do then? Whom should you talk to first? Most people say Realtor 3, because he or she thinks the property can sell for the highest amount. Wrong! That is just chasing money. I'd rather protect it first. I call Realtor 1 and find out why he or she thinks the property will only sell for $350,000. Sometimes you will get a really good reason, such as "The views are all going away, as they are closing the park and building an apartment complex directly behind the house" or "A gang of armed vigilantes just moved in next door and are harassing the neighborhood and painting their house neon green." Okay, the second scenario may be extreme, but you get the point. However, the realtor may have a response such as "Have you seen the house? It's ugly, it's a mess!." That's when you remind the realtor that you are going to fix it up and you are trying to determine what it can sell for *after* it has been repaired. If you get an answer like that, you know the realtor didn't really do his or her job and you can dismiss the $350,000 response.

As real estate investors, we use the term "after-repair value" or ARV. Realtors might package their valuations in different words, such as broker's price opinion (BPO), comparative market analysis (CMA), or list price. What it comes down to is you want to find out what they think it will actually sell for, not what they think you can list it at. No matter how many opinions of value you get from realtors, remember, get *proof* of and *support* for why they think their values are correct.

3. **Take an average price of recently sold proper-ties.** I see investors using this method a lot. An average is not a definitive way to determine an ARV. For example, let's say there are six recent sales in the neighborhood:

House 1 sold for $200,000

House 2 sold for $209,500

House 3 sold for $210,000

House 4 sold for $219,900

House 5 sold for $222,000

House 6 sold for $245,000

Add up the six sales prices and you get $1,306,400. Then divide by the number of properties (6), and you get the average price of $217,733.33. So you should be able to safely say that your house should be able to sell at $217,000, right? Wrong. What if your house doesn't have a garage, and house 1 is the only similar one, and houses 2–6 all have two- and three-car garages? Or pools. Or larger square footage. Or back onto golf courses and have views. Or have any number of other special value-added features. If your property is most similar to house 1 and you overvalued your ARV by $17,000, get ready to lose money. Let's look at it in reverse. What if your house has a three-car garage and a pool and you are going to install that golden toilet? Maybe house 6 has all of these features as well, and your ARV should be closer to $245,000. If you based your offer price on an ARV of $217,000, you probably offered too low, and someone else got the deal instead of you, because he or she used a more accurate ARV. The ARV pendulum swings both ways. A bad ARV can get you into bad deals *or* it can make you miss out on good deals.

4. **Take an average price per foot of the recently sold properties.** Again, I often see investors and other real estate professionals using this method. An average is not a definitive way to determine an ARV. For example, let's say there are six recent sales in the neighborhood:

   House 1 sold for $200,000 at 1,400 square feet = $142.86/ square foot

   House 2 sold for $209,500 at 1,157 square feet = $181.07/ square foot

   House 3 sold for $210,000 at 1,482 square feet = $141.70/ square foot

   House 4 sold for $219,900 at 1,585 square feet = $138.74/ square foot

   House 5 sold for $222,000 at 1,954 square feet = $113.61/ square foot

   House 6 sold for $245,000 at 1,400 square feet = $175.00/ square foot

Add up the six price-per-square-foot figures, and you get $892.98. Then, divide by the number of properties (6), and you get the average price per foot of $148.83. So you should be able to safely say that your 1,500-square-foot house should be able to sell at $223,245, right? Wrong. Again, these type of equations do not take into account variances such as garages, pools, views, and that golden toilet! Houses 1 and 6 are the same square footage, but sold with a $45,000 price differential. Maybe house 6 backs up to a lake and the $45,000 difference in value can be attributed to that? If your house does back up to a lake and you based your offer price on an ARV of $223,245, you probably offered too low, and someone else got the deal instead of you, because he or she used a more accurate ARV. Or, if the house doesn't have a lake view, you offered too high and got a bad deal. However, price per foot can be used to find potential deals. If I saw house 1 and house 6 both listed for sale at those prices, and they were the same square footage and model matches to each other, I would think that there was potential there for profit on house 1, but I would delve into *why* there was such a price difference by using a more accurate approach to determining ARV. Use your tools correctly.

I also see real estate professionals try to determine an ARV of a property using this price-per-square-foot method when the property is of a larger square footage than everything else around it. The six properties listed above have a range of 1,157sf up to 1,954sf. But what happens if you have a 2,800sf and there are no recent sales of similar properties of that same size? Some people will than use the average price per foot of $148.83 and multiply the 2,800sf to determine their ARV, in this case it would be $416,724. It doesn't work this way, just don't do it.

5. Find the highest sale in the neighborhood and use that. Don't fall into the trap of thinking "I know my house is going to be the best one in the neighborhood when it is done, so I can price it at the top of the market." Just because it's been remodeled, doesn't necessarily mean it has the same features, location, or appeal as the property that sold at the highest price. Should a correctly remodeled property get a top-dollar price? Yes, but a 1,500-square-foot house typically does not sell at the same top-dollar price of a 2,000-square-foot house. You have to look for similar properties and compare your property to those. Realtors love saying things like "Houses in this neighborhood have sold for over $400,000!." If your house is not the same as those houses, chances are you aren't going to sell in that same price range.

6. **Use a Zillow estimated value.** Even as I type this, I am shaking my head. If you go to Zillow, it reports, "Nationally, the Zestimate has a median error rate of 5.4% which means half of the Zestimates in an area are closer than the error percentage and half are farther off." If I am putting a few hundred thousand dollars on the line, heck, if I am only putting a few thousand dollars on the line, I am going to want something more convincing than "about half the time we are only off by 5.4%." I've had properties for which Zillow has been off by more than 50%. Zillow can be a good source for information, but if you are looking for an ARV, stay clear of Zillow.

7. **Order an appraisal.** An appraisal is a method to value a property and is completed by a local expert who is trained and licensed in his or her state and should be able to give a reasonably accurate opinion of value. Notice the key word "opinion." An appraisal is not a definitive, end-all valuation, especially if you don't give the appraiser the

necessary information to correctly formulate his or her opinion. What type of information will an appraiser need? Well, for starters, you need to find an appraiser who has some experience in *forecasting*, as you really are looking for a *"future value"* on a *"subject to appraisal."* Did you all get that?

Don't worry if you didn't, because most appraisers who are reading this didn't get it either. Forecasting means they are going to try to foretell the future. Looking at past and current market trends, current inventory levels, and a few other indicators, a highly trained appraiser can, with a certain level of accuracy, determine what a property's value should be in the near future, say 2–4 months from the time of appraisal, it's *"future value"*. Now, take it to the next step: *"subject to appraisal."* What does that mean? It means the appraiser is not going to value the property in its current condition, he or she is going to value it *subject to* the repairs you are planning on making. Guess what? If you don't give the appraiser the exact breakdown on what you are doing to the property, it will affect the final opinion of the value. If you say, "I am going to put granite countertops in the house and tile flooring and also paint," the appraiser may value it with high-end granite throughout, highly upgraded tile flooring, and brand-new interior and exterior paint. But what if you only put a low-end granite in the kitchen, a cheap tile flooring in one room, and only paint the inside? Do you think that might affect the final value? Although most appraisers do not know what ARV means, they should at least understand the concept to some degree. However, due to government regulations since the previous market crash, appraisers overall have become more cautious in their valuations. This means they are coming in at lower value opinions to protect themselves. In the end, an appraisal is just an opinion, and unless you are providing an extensive amount of information to the appraiser and he or she is one of the few appraisers actually trained to do these type of appraisals, his or her opinion is going to be just as good as that of a realtor, but you will have to pay for the appraisal. Don't buy appraisals!

8. **Ask the homeowner what the property is worth.**
   This is right up there with using Zillow estimates. If you are trying to buy anything, don't ask the person who is selling it what he or she thinks it is worth! Every homeowner thinks his or her home is made out of gold and is the best, because he or she wants to get the most amount of money possible from the sale. A homeowner is not an expert in determining ARVs; that's your job. Yes, people actually teach this method and the other seven listed here (and more for that matter). If you are asking a homeowner for a value, and you base your offer price on that, do you think there might be an issue?

Okay, so we covered multiple ways to *not* determine ARV, but within some of those *do nots*, there are little things that you should do. Now it's time to tell you how to actually determine ARV. When you can start determining your ARVs more accurately, you will get into safe real estate investments and make money! The first thing you need to understand is the concept of *comparable sales*. Comparable sales are recently sold properties similar in features, appeal and location to your subject property.

Here are my criteria for determining whether a sale is a comparable sale and how I use them to determine ARV:

1. Only use sales that have sold within the past 180 days (preferably in the past 90 days). List prices are a hope and a dream. A recorded sales price is a fact. A comparable sale must be a closed sale, not an active listing, pending sale, or contingent sale.

2. Comparable sales should be remodeled or well-maintained, move-in ready properties. Don't use foreclosures, short sale, or other distressed properties.

3. Similar design. This is for looks and functionality. Use apple-to-apple comparisons; it's okay if it is a Granny Smith to your MacIntosh, but it shouldn't be a banana to a mango. A two-bedroom home will never be the same as a four-bedroom home. A one-story house will never be the same as two-story house. If you are the only banana in a neighborhood of peaches, move on to the next potential deal. If you are a new investor, I do not recommend you go after the oddball properties, the properties with negative market factors such as being adjacent to a busy road, the only house in the neighborhood without a garage or with some other attribute that makes it truly unique. These types of properties have fewer potential buyers and therefore take longer to sell. Stick to apples.

4. Use a minimum of three comparable sales to determine your ARV.

5. Same market area, no further than 1 mile, and not on the other side of a major highway, traffic artery, or natural barrier like a river or lake.

6. Square footage should be within 15% of your property and room count should be similar (always think apple to apple). If you have a 2,000-square-foot house, you should be looking at properties in the range of 1,700–2,300 square feet.

7. Only use sales from the local MLS—it is the best resource.

So where do you get the comparable sales from? I will have three Realtors send me a list of the recent sales that match the above criteria and I will look through those lists and pick out the 3 to 5 most similar properties. These are my comparable sales. Properties that match my above criteria as close as possible, apples to my apple. Once you have your comparable sales, you need to look at them and decide which one is the best, the most similar.

Subject property: 1,422 square feet, one story, two-car garage, built in 1987, three bedrooms/two bathrooms

Comparable sale 1: 1,504 square feet, one story, two-car garage, built in 1988, three bedrooms/two bathrooms; sold for $245,000 on August 10, 2016

Comparable sale 2: 1,387 square feet, one story, one-car garage, built in 1982, three bedrooms/two bathrooms; sold for $227,000 on September 15, 2016

Comparable sale 3: 1,450 square feet, one story, two-car garage, built in 1991, three bedrooms/two bathrooms; sold for $249,000 on July 17, 2016

Comparable sale 4: 1,334 square feet, one story, one-car garage, built in 1982, three bedrooms/two bathrooms; sold for $235,000 on June 22, 2016

Comparable sale 5: 1,422 square feet, one story, two-car garage, built in 1986, three bedrooms/two bathrooms; sold for $242,000 on July 30, 2016

When you look at the five comparable sales, it is important not only to look at their stat lines, their property details, but also to look at their pictures. Your realtor should be able to send you a link to the MLS listing sheets so you can read the marketing descriptions and review the marketing photographs. Properties that are in good condition or recently remodeled will almost always have pictures in the MLS or online to showcase them. If a property only has exterior pictures, you can typically assume the inside was not in great shape. Based on what my subject property has and knowing that I am going to do a pretty thorough remodel and I have a model match (comparable 5) that sold for $242,000, I would place my ARV at $245,000. Could it sell for more? There is a very similar house in comparable sale 3 that sold for $249,000. Yes, it could, but I am not going to top out my ARV. If it sells for more than $245,000, that is just icing on the cake. So why did I not select an ARV of $235,000? The lower-priced homes were a little older and only had one-car garages. Comparable sales 1, 3, and 5 are the most similar and should be given the most weight, the most consideration. Always find the most similar properties and give the most consideration to the best apple in the bunch. This is the same method an appraiser is supposed to use, and that is why it is the best way. Why is that important? Because when you go to sell your house after it is remodeled, the buyers will be getting a loan that will be contingent on an appraisal. It doesn't matter if John and Jane Homebuyer are willing to pay you $285,000 for your house if the house will only appraise at $245,000. They won't be able to qualify for a loan, and most buyers are not willing to or cannot come up with an additional $40,000 out of pocket when a professional has told them the house isn't worth it. We'll talk more on that when we discuss contracts and offers in later chapters. Calculate your ARV the way an appraiser is supposed to. Calculate it using facts and data, apple-to-apple comparisons, and a complete understanding of what your rehabbed property is going to be. Knowing how to determine your ARV is the most vital aspect of flipping a house. Your ARV is truly the most important number in any real estate transaction.

Now that you have comparables and a good sense of what your ARV is, let's consider whether you should even do this deal. Although we looked at the days on market for your market area, you still need to always look at the DOM of your comparables. If all of the comparables you used to determine your ARV took more than 90 days to sell, guess what? Your property will probably take more than 90 days to sell too! This means more holding costs and more time for something to go wrong. Just because you have a solid ARV doesn't mean you should do the deal. I want the average DOM of my comparables to also be less than 60 days. This means my house is a desired type of house in a desired market. You want your properties to move fast! The faster you can sell a house, the quicker you get your profit. The faster you sell your house, the happier your investors will be (we'll talk more about investors in chapter 6).

Now let's talk about how you can estimate repair costs. You want to use a repair estimate when you develop your offer price. Using an estimate gets your foot in the door that much faster than those investors who walk a property with a contractor and wait for a bid. You can have an offer to a seller the day it is listed, while other investors might take a week. So how should you estimate your repairs? Some seminars will give you a breakdown on how much a bathroom should cost, how much a door costs, how much a new window costs. This method can work, but it can be rather time-consuming, and most likely you are not an expert in construction. You may not know if you need new valves in your shower, you may not know you need a support beam if you are removing a load-bearing wall, you may not know if you need a new header above your new windows. I prefer estimating my repairs based on two factors:

1. The square footage of the house (this is the heated and/ or cooled area of the house, the livable area and does not include garage areas).

2. The extent of the remodel and the current condition of the house. If the house is in decent shape already, it needs less work. If a house has been vandalized, it's going to need a lot more work.

After flipping houses across the country and talking with many real estate investors in multiple markets, I developed a baseline for these varying scenarios. More often than not the rehab is within a couple thousand dollars of this estimated number. Here are the four categories I break my rehabs down into:

1. "Lipstick" or rental remodels. These will typically run you about $14 per square foot of your property. This is if you have a dirty or dated house and you are just needing to replace items like carpet, paint, appliances, countertops, and fixtures to basically make everything clean, in working order, and livable.

2. "Standard" remodels. These will typically run you about $18 per square foot. You are going to be doing a bit more, such as installing hard-surface flooring, new showers, and new cabinets; opening up a wall; and maybe replacing a larger item, such as a roof or pool resurface.

3. "Vandalized" remodels. These will typically be a little more than your standard remodel, as you may need to replace stolen copper wiring and piping, repair drywall that is broken or smashed in multiple places, and/or replace mechanical systems that are damaged or missing. These will typically run you about $26 per square foot.

4. "Upgraded" remodels. This is your next-level house, in which you need to add some extra touches and nicer finishes, such as travertine stone flooring; upgraded, built-in appliances; crown moldings; and other high-end details. Remember, the comparables will tell you what level you need to do. Upgraded remodels will typically be around $32 per square foot.

How do you figure out which of these four categories your flip falls into? Look at the pictures of your subject property and the comparables! You have to know how much you need to do and then make it just a little bit better than your comparables. Notice I am not telling you to go walk the property and kick the tires. 99% of the offers I make are on properties I have not even been inside of. Save that for your due diligence time period when your offer gets accepted. The pictures should give you enough of an idea of what you need or don't need. Most of the gurus teach that you must always do this repair or that repair. I've spoken with many new investors who are either fresh from these seminars or are just avid watchers of the reality television shows about flipping houses, and they typically overestimate their repairs, usually because they want to over improve the property. If your repair estimate is too high, then your offers will be too low! I had one investor ask me to review a deal for which he had just put in an offer. He had estimated more than $60,000 in repairs on a 1,700-square-foot property. He was basically replacing everything on the inside and all of the mechanical systems; this was beyond the $32 per square foot for an upgraded remodel. Something didn't sound right to me. I looked at the pictures of the subject property. It was currently being lived in and was pretty dirty, borderline gross, and also needed some updating. I then looked at the comparables and saw that these houses had some nice features; however, overall, they were just clean, ready to move-in houses, not the "flips" you see on television, where everything is new and shiny. Since the subject property was actively being lived in, you can typically assume the mechanical systems are all working and at most need servicing, not replacing. The investor had budgeted in high-end appliances, new windows, and upgraded solid-surface flooring throughout. The comparables didn't have new windows. If none of my comparables have new windows and all of my subject property's windows are functioning and working, why would I spend the $4,000 to replace them? That is just wasting your money. Although these additional repairs and upgrades will make a nicer house, you won't make any additional money. This is called a *cost–benefit analysis*. It's the process of determining whether or not it makes sense to do certain repairs and what you will get in return. A simple cost–benefit analysis is replacing stained and dirty carpet. Will the house sell at a higher price with new carpet? In most markets yes, not only will it sell for a higher amount, but it will have more potential buyers, thus increasing the demand for the property. There can be multiple benefits associated with cost items. As I went through the comparable sales for this property, I noticed most of them had carpet in the bedrooms and living areas and either tile or vinyl flooring in the wet areas (wet areas are places with faucets—bathrooms, kitchens, laundry rooms, etc.). The investor was budgeting for a high-end tile throughout the entire living area, with a wood flooring going into the bedrooms. He told me it was going to be beautiful. I agreed with him that it would be beautiful, but I also told him it was going to be a waste of money, he was over improving the property! He was estimating the repairs beyond an upgraded remodel, when all the property needed was a lipstick remodel. The house really only needed carpet, tile, countertops, fixtures, and appliances. There was no benefit to the added costs, the over improvements. He ended up not getting this house because his offer was too low. Another investor ended up getting it, paid more than the others had offered, did a lipstick remodel, and sold it for a nice profit. Know what your market requires and review the comparables you are using to determine your ARV.

I'm not saying you should be cheap and put out bad products. If you put lipstick on a pig, it's still a pig. When you flip a house, everything needs to be working and the property should be livable and move-in ready. You can still do nice features in a house, but only go slightly nicer than the comparables, because this will make the house sell faster and typically at top dollar. However, don't go overboard. Remember, this is a business, and we are not making emotional decisions on our rehabs. The most important thing in repairs is to know what to do or not do. I always over improve my properties a little bit, as that way I know that my house will be more desirable than anything else out there, will sell faster, and will be more likely to be appraised at or above the contract price, and overall I will make more money doing this! If you don't do enough, the house will sit, and not many people will want it; if you do too much, people will want it, but it most likely won't be appraised at the contract price and will still sell at the same price it would without the extras, and you will make less profit. An extra $1,000 to upgrade granite and plumbing fixtures might be what it takes to sell your house 1 month faster! It's worth it. A $1,000 light fixture that you love and that will look amazing in the dining room of a $100,000 house is probably not a good business decision. The four rehab levels given above are your starting points to determine your estimated repair numbers, the numbers you use to make your offers. When time is of the essence and you want to make a quick offer, having a method to determine solid repair estimates is key. What if your repair estimate is wrong? Don't sweat it. Once you have a property under contract you will go into your due diligence time period. During this time, you will have actual contractors go to the property and get you quotes for the actual repairs. Your estimates are a way to calculate an offer and get your foot in the door.

Now that you have your ARV and an estimate of your needed repairs, what do you do with them? How do you start making offers? Where is the magic formula these gurus talk about? Sorry to tell you, but there is no magic formula, no matter what the gurus teach. Making offers based on 50–75% of ARV doesn't work. I've bought deals ranging from 30–84% of ARV, but I didn't use a magic formula to figure out how to make these deals happen. I used basic math. You just have to know the figures you need. Here are the blanks you need to fill in, in the most basic terms possible:

After-repair value

    –   Closing costs at purchase (approx. 2% of Purchase Price)

- Repair estimate

- Holding costs (estimate $200–500 per month for taxes, utilities, insurance, and home owner associations, and then plan for a 6-month project minimum)

- Loan costs (*if needed*—typically around 7% of your ARV for a hard money loan)

- Closing costs at sale (8% of ARV should cover standard realtor costs and title/escrow fees)

- Desired profit (beginners should go for 15% of ARV, but not less than $20,000)

    = Maximum purchase price

- So let's go with our example we used earlier of the 1,422-square-foot house with an ARV of $245,000 but listed for $150,000.

- $245,000 (ARV)

- $3,000 (purchase closing costs 2% of purchase price, use the list price to estimate this)

- $25,596 ($18 per square foot for a standard remodel)

- $3,000 (always budget for 6 months of holding costs, $500 × 6)

- $17,150 (7% of ARV for hard money loan costs—if you need it)

- $19,600 (8% for sale closing costs to pay realtors and title/escrow)

- $36,750 (15% of ARV for desired profit)

= $139,904 maximum offer price

If I offered $139,904 and this deal went six months, I would stand to profit approximately $36,750. However, on a property like this I would start my offer in the $130,000 to $135,000, knowing that I had a little wiggle room if they tried to negotiate. Please do not make offers at $139,904—realtors and sellers will know you are just plugging into some type of formula and you aren't truly serious. Round your offer price to the nearest thousand. You don't want to offer so low that you don't get the house though. I've had students who wanted to offer $110,000 on a house like this. The further from the list price you go, the lower your chances of getting the offer accepted. I've also had students who wanted to offer $155,000 on this same house, just so they could get their first deal. They said they would be okay with a $10,000 profit on it. They were letting their emotions take control. They wanted that first deal so badly, they were going to put their money at risk. There are other deals out there, do not be so eager that you get hurt!

The "no formula" formula is just simple math. Each market will vary a little for items such as closing costs and carrying costs, but it's always best to plan for a little bit more than you expect. Pad your numbers. If someone gives you an estimate of $200–300, use the higher number. Even though it is just simple math, it will still take time to feel comfortable running these numbers and believing in them. You will have doubts, you will question whether you are right. Do not let that doubt keep you from taking action and making offers! What Wayne Gretzky said about hockey applies in real estate as well: you will miss 100% of the offers you don't make.

CHAPTER 3 FLIP TIPS

1. The after-repair value, ARV, is the single most important number in a deal.

2. Comparable sales criteria to determine ARV:

   a. Must be closed sales in that were closed in the past 180 days—don't use pending/contingent sales or active listings.

   b. Properties should be clean, move-in ready, or preferably flipped properties.

   c. Compare apples to apples (consider design and appeal—a one-story ranch is not the same as a two-story subdivision house).

   d. Minimum of three closed sales to determine your ARV.

   e. Within 1 mile, but not on the other side of a highway or natural barrier.

   f. Gross living area ±15%.

   g. Only use sales from your local MLS, which is the best data source.

3. Repairs: lipstick or rental remodels = $14 per square foot; standard remodels = $18 per square foot; vandalized remodels = $26 per square foot; upgraded remodels = $32 per square foot.

4. A repair estimate is a way to get your foot in the door before everyone else.

5. A picture is worth 1,000 hours, don't waste your time walking every property. Look at the pictures and determine your repairs from your desk.

6. There is no magic formula.

7. You have to make offers to get offers accepted.

CHAPTER 4 –

The Overflowing Inbox

Many investors think finding deals is the hardest part of this business. Most of the time it's because they are only looking in one place and in one way. There are deals all around you, you just have to know how to find them and make sure you aren't closing any doors. Throughout my real estate investing career I have grown and created the ways I now find deals so that I now have an over-flowing inbox, something that you can have too. I am always having other investors ask me where I get my deals. My answer is usually the same: "Anywhere and everywhere." That sounds kind of like the generic brush-off answer someone would give you if he or she really didn't want to share information, right? It is. Let me give you the real answers. The main source for my deals over the past 6 years has been the multiple listing service, the MLS. This is the realtor database in which realtors list homes that are for sale and are available for other realtors to see. Even though only licensed realtors have direct access to this resource, it is still considered to be on the open market, mean-ing anyone can typically buy these listings. Most real estate websites, such as Zillow and Redfin, pull their data from MLS systems. The majority of residential real estate sales and purchases in the United States occur in the MLS. Properties that are listed for sale within the MLS can be listings from private sellers, banks, short sales, and even new-construction homes. The MLS is the single best data tool for market statistics, determining ARVs, and finding properties to purchase, and this is why you need multiple realtors on your team. Realtors who know how to do custom searches, keyword searches, and auto searches within their MLS systems. Each MLS system has its own nuances, but the biggest cities in the country typically have very functional and useful search options. I have my realtors set up auto searches in their MLS systems. What this means is they set up my criteria once and then save the search. I like to compare it to fishing. I am having the realtor put lines in the water; if a fish (a listing that fits my search criteria) comes up and nibbles at the line, the MLS sends the realtor and me an automatic email notification. Once I receive that email, I do my research, my realtor knows to send me comparable sales that fit my criteria, and I decide whether I want to make an offer and reel that fish in! The more automated you can make this business, the better. You shouldn't expect your realtor to just search nonstop every day in the MLS for properties. Realtors have better things to do, so make your business more efficient, so they want to keep working for you. My top three auto searches are these:

The Dirty Dozen. This is my keyword auto search. Naming it the Dirty Dozen gives it more credibility when you are first starting out with a new realtor; it makes it look like you have a system in place that has worked in other markets and you are expanding it to include the new realtor. The Dirty Dozen is twelve words that typically mean the property is distressed or a fixer-upper. The realtor will set up this auto search for any active listing that has one of these words or phrases in the listing:

1. Distressed

2. Fixer

3. Repairs

4. Tool belt

5. Handyman

6. Must sell

7. Reduced

8. BOM (this will stand for either back on market or bottom of market)

9. Damaged

10. Fixer-upper

11. Short sale approved

12. Do not enter

I have my realtors set the Dirty Dozen auto search for the entire MLS. I do not limit this to just one zip code or one area, or even to just single family homes. I let my realtors know I will buy anything I can make money on. Realtors are typically used to dealing with individual home buyers driven by need and emotion. Individual home buyers have to be in a certain school district or they have to be close to their office or they must have four bedrooms or they must have a pool. The list is endless. I, as an investor, just need deals I can make money on. When a realtor tells me, and they do, "You don't want to be over in that part of town, it's a bad area." I simply ask, "Can I make money over there? I'm sure I can. I will buy anything I can make money on." They may just be saying it because they aren't familiar with the area, they don't want to drive that far, or they are biased for one reason or another. Let the data tell you where you want to be, not the realtors.

REO search. REO stands for "real estate owned" and is used to describe properties owned by banks, lenders, or government agencies for properties they have taken back through foreclosure. I don't want my realtor to send me every REO in the MLS. If an REO property is just listed and needs repairs, it will typically have one of the Dirty Dozen in it, so you will catch it on that line. However, a lot of REO properties get repaired by the banks, as they know they have a broader purchaser base for a ready to move-in house than a house that needs repairs, and therefore they can make more money on it. Additionally, many banks and government entities will have sale restrictions on their properties and won't even consider an offer from a nonoccupant (that's you, the real estate investor) for the first

30 days it is listed. They do this so that John and Jane Homebuyer can compete and find a house, but they also do this because they know John and Jane Homebuyer will typically pay more than a real estate investor. *Everyone* does cost–benefit analysis in this business. Although many REO properties are not good flips because they have already been remodeled, or they may have restrictions on who can actually buy them, some REO properties can be lucrative. My Dirty Dozen search will be the first fishing lines in the water, but I want my realtors to set up a few more. I want my realtors to direct their focus toward REO properties that have been listed for sale for 44 days. The reason why I go with 44 days is because banks typically have a method in dropping their prices. They will typically do their first price drop at 30 or 31 days from the initial listing, with a following price drop 2 weeks later or at 45 days. I like to get my offer out to them just before the second price drop. The property has been sitting on the market for a while, it's due for a price drop, and they get my offer? Reel that fish in! The longer an REO property has been listed on the MLS, the more likely it is the bank will take a lowball offer just to offload it. You can set up another auto search for 59 days as well. Make sure you look at the listing history of the properties before you offer too low, as sometimes the property may have been previously under contract and then was relisted due to the prior buyer not being able to close. Again, I will have the realtor set these searches for the entire MLS area.

Price per square foot for market area. This is where you have to narrow your MLS area down and look at a more defined neighborhood approach to properties. This is a way to find motivated sellers, people who want to sell a house and sell it fast. I will tell the realtor to pick out neighborhoods and do the following search:

1. Map the neighborhood boundaries (MLS systems typically have a drawing tool the realtor can use to draw a shape around the neighborhood of interest).

2. Search for single-family homes sold in the past 90 days that were not distressed, meaning no REO or short sale properties (again, most MLS systems will allow the realtor to remove these property types from the search criteria with a click of a button).

3. Find the sales price per square foot of the sold properties only.

4. Set an auto search for the mapped boundaries at 80% and below of the price per square foot. This means that if houses within the mapped boundaries have been selling at $100 per square foot over the past 90 days, I want the realtor to set up an auto search for any listings that are at $80 per square foot or less. If everyone else is selling his or her house at $200,000, and someone lists a similarly sized house at $160,000, do you think that person is motivated? I do, and I want to see that house! I want to buy houses from motivated sellers, not sellers who want top dollar for their properties. That same neighborhood could have an REO property of similar size listed at $209,000. While other investors are looking at the one that is priced too high by an unrealistic seller, I am looking at the $160,000 property and making my offer on that! Again, the realtor's auto search will send both of us an email with the property. I train my realtors to send comparables for any of the properties that come up in the auto searches; that way I have all the information I need, I can come up with my ARV, estimate my repairs, and send them my offer!

I buy all types of properties out of the MLS. I buy REOs, short sales, and traditional sales (those sales listed by the actual homeowner). As I said earlier, I tell my realtors that I will buy anything I can make money on. I do the same searches for condominiums and townhouses that I do for single-family homes. I buy anything I can make money on. While other investors are limiting their earning potential by stating they only want to be in this zip code, or they will only buy houses built after 1980 or they will only buy houses with garages. I am buying anything and everything that I can make money on. I know I have repeated it multiple times in this section, but being open to all deals has truly helped me get to where I am now.

Another reason why you need multiple realtors on your team is because realtors will get off-market deals they can send your way. We call these *pocket listings*. A pocket listing is a listing the realtor has been given by a homeowner or a bank but has *not* put it in the MLS yet; they are basically giving you the first crack at it. Sometimes they are doing it just because they like you or they think that you are serious and will truly purchase the property and make their job easier. Other times they are doing it because they want to make double the commission. This means they are representing the seller in the sale of the house and they are representing you, the buyer, in the purchase of the house. Sometimes they may even tell you that they will give it to you only if you let them list it. At the typical commission rate of 3% per side of a transaction, this realtor will stand to make three separate commissions. If the purchase price is $200,000, the realtor will make 6% or $12,000 by representing both you and the seller. If he or she sells the finished property for you at $300,000, the realtor will make another $9,000, for a total of $21,000 on the deal. Not bad, right? But who cares what they make, you need to just care about your numbers and whether the deal works for you. I know some investors who would tell a realtor to take a hike if this offer was presented to them. If it is a deal, it's a deal. Don't begrudge the realtor his or her hustle. Never complain about what somebody else makes in a transaction if your numbers work for you. The more realtors you connect with, the more chances you will have at getting pocket deals presented to you.

Although realtors are the main way I get most of my houses, I do get houses from other sources as well. The second-highest source for my projects is wholesalers. A wholesaler is someone who puts a property under contract and then sells you his or her interest in the contract. A wholesaler is basically a property finder. There are some really good wholesalers out there, but there are a lot of really bad ones too. With most wholesalers, you should never trust their ARVs and you should never trust their repair numbers. A lot of times they will even have the address wrong! But I do love wholesalers, and I have paid wholesalers more than $1 million in the past 3 years to bring me properties. I have paid amounts from $1,000 to $60,000, and I know other investors who have paid wholesalers more than $200,000 for a single deal! Is that crazy? Not if the deal still works for you. I paid one wholesaler $37,000 on a deal I only made $18,000 on. Did I care that the wholesaler made more than me? Not at all. I was happy with the $18,000, the deal worked for me, and I bought it. I told the wholesaler to send me more! This is what I tell my wholesalers: "I don't care what you make on a deal, the numbers just have to work for me. All I need from you is the address, *my* price, and pictures if you have them." Just as I do with my realtors, I try to keep it simple for my wholesalers. Why ask them what they think the repairs are going to be when you know you can't trust their numbers? The reason why I phrase it as "*my* price," is that some wholesalers will give you their contract prices and their assignment fees (the amount they are making on the deal) separately. For example, I want the wholesaler to just tell me my price is $150,000, I don't need to know the wholesaler has it under contract for $140,000 and the assignment fee is $10,000. If I need to go back to that wholesaler and tell him or her the deal doesn't work for me at $150,000, but it does at $142,000, which number do you suspect the wholesaler thinks I am reducing? The assignment fee, of course! If I don't know what the fee is, the wholesaler won't think I am just trying to take $8,000 out of his or her pocket. Is a wholesaler really worth $2,000? $10,000? $200,000? You need to understand what a wholesaler does to answer that question. Wholesaler typically mail out lots of letters and postcards to distressed sellers, they drive around neighborhoods and knock on doors of damaged-looking houses, they post what we call "bandit signs" on street corners. A bandit sign typically reads something like "I want to buy your house for cash, call me." These signs, more often than not, are posted by wholesalers, not flippers. I call any of these bandit signs I see and ask the wholesalers to sell me properties. I have connected with many wholesalers this way. Wholesalers may go through 100 or 200 potential deals before they get one that they can even send you. They listen to sob story after sob story, they are threatened by irate homeowners, and they receive their mailings returned to them with nasty notes from homeowners. So yes, in my opinion, the wholesaler is worth whatever he or she can make ... as long as the deal still works for me, of course. The wholesaler is the used-car salesperson of the real estate world. If you want a used car, where do you go?

There are all different places to connect with wholesalers. The number one location in any market is typically Craigslist.com. There is a bit of a game that gets played in the wholesale real estate world, and as long as you have an understanding of the game, you can play.

Wholesalers are on Craigslist typically to just build their buyer lists. You are the buyer, an investor who is looking for properties to fix and flip. The wholesaler will typically put an ad in the "real estate for sale by owner" section of Craigslist. This property will be too good to be true. The wholesaler will typically title it using words like "fixer-upper" or "perfect flip" or "$50,000 profit." The truth of the matter is that 99% of the time the wholesaler does not actually have a house for sale. When you contact him or her, either by email or phone, he or she will tell you: "That property just sold, but let me get your name and number, and the next one I get, I'll give you a call." This is typically followed up by the wholesaler asking you what your buying criteria are, what zip code you want to be in, what price point, and so on. I tell them the same thing I tell my realtors, "I buy anything I can make money on. If you think it is a deal, just send it to me." You will also find more honest ads on Craigslist; those are typically from wholesalers who direct you to their website to sign up for their super-secret, priority buyer, amazing person group. You want to connect with all of the wholesalers in your market area.

This should be a continual thing in your business, and you should spend 30 minutes per week on Craigslist just connecting with wholesalers. The more lists you are on, the better your chance of getting a deal. Additionally, the more wholesalers you talk to, the better you will get at speaking with them. Wholesalers, just like house flippers, have seminars and education courses they can attend and study, and most of the wholesalers on Craigslist are new to the business. On the flip side of things, I will also post my own ads on Craigslist in the same section as the wholesalers. The purpose of my ad is to let wholesalers know that I am looking to buy properties. I will typically title my ad something along the lines of "Flipper Needs More Properties" and I will have the description read something like "I am looking to buy more fix and flip properties. Wholesalers, send me your deals. I am a cash buyer. All I need from you is the address, *my* price, and pictures if you have them." I will also post one picture with this ad, typically I will use a picture of a damaged interior room or a remodeled room. You will get more responses to your ads if you include a picture. If you have never done a Craigslist ad, now is the time. Put this book down, place your ad, and start connecting with wholesalers.

You can also connect with wholesalers at local real estate–investing meet-up groups. I will also connect with national wholesalers on Facebook and LinkedIn. We'll talk more about social media and networking in chapter 11. Just know that the more people you connect with, the more deals you will find, the more money you will find, the more everything you will find.

Once I get a deal from my wholesaler, I give the address to my realtor and ask for some comparables and ask what the realtor thinks I can sell it for after I fix it up. Why would your realtor do this? Because he or she thinks you are the cat's meow? No, a realtor does this in the hope of getting the future listing from you. You are dangling a carrot in front of the realtor to get what you need. Make sure to let him or her know this is urgent, because I can guarantee the wholesaler is putting the same deal in front of other buyers. Buying properties from wholesalers is not the same as buying properties from a realtor in the MLS. Typically, wholesalers want you to complete all of your research, your due diligence, beforehand, and they require you to give them a nonrefundable earnest money deposit, or EMD, once you have signed a contract with them. Some wholesalers will ask for this EMD in cash or as a check made out directly to the wholesaler, but I don't do that. I always place my EMD with a title/escrow company, as I want to keep my money safe. The wholesaler will typically give you the opportunity to walk the property before putting it under contract. I recommend you take a contractor with you on these walks, take a lot of pictures, and really run your numbers. If you back out after you have put in your EMD, don't plan on getting your EMD back from a wholesaler. Additionally, a lot of the paperwork that wholesalers use is meant to only protect the wholesaler, not the seller and not you, the buyer. The typical wholesaler will have the seller sign a purchase agreement and this will name the wholesaler as the buyer, but gives him or her the right to assign the contract to another person or entity. Once the wholesaler finds a buyer (that's you), the wholesaler signs an assignment agreement with you, which transfers his or her rights and interests in the original contract over to you for a fee. Do not sign an assignment agreement without reading the original purchase agreement. You want to know what terms are being assigned to you and what you are agreeing to! What if the seller and the wholesaler agreed that the seller could rent the property back for up to 6 months at $200 per month? You might want to know about that before you agree to anything. Always read your paperwork.

A lot of new investors get really excited about buying houses from auctions. It sounds like a sexy and exhilarating thing to do. But we do not let emotion control our decisions, and a lot of people get carried away at auctions. I personally love auctions and have bought many houses at them. I love going to silent auctions for charities, and I bid on everything I can. I understand the thrill of winning something, but with housing auctions you need to stick to your numbers. Just because someone else is willing to pay more than you, doesn't mean it's worth it for you. Maybe he or she didn't run the numbers correctly, maybe he or she has a different exit strategy. Stick to your numbers, have your maximum bid, and do not go over it. Just as when dealing with wholesalers, most auctions do not have a due diligence time period after you have won the auction. However, many auctions do have preview periods before the auctions when you can view the properties, run your numbers, establish your ARV, and even take contractors on a walkthrough. These are all important steps to complete before bidding, because once you have won that auction, you typically are now on the hook for the property. The thrill of the auction can be addictive; it feels good to win. I once had to help an investor who won thirty-four properties at auction in a 2-week time span. Thirty-four properties in five different states. When he came to me, he had already placed his EMDs with the auction house and had closings scheduled for the next week. He was very excited and proud of all of these great deals he had gotten. He started showing me the deals, and I began asking questions. Where are the comparables you used for your ARVs? Did your realtor walk the properties? Where are your pictures? Where are your contractor bids? He looked at me blankly. His due diligence had consisted of pulling sales data from Zillow, his realtors had never been to the properties, and he had never even contacted a contractor for repair bids. He had sent his EMD in on all of these properties, but he didn't have the funds to close any of these properties! This story is real. I spent the next 3 days helping this investor analyze deals, contact realtors, review comparables, and determine ARVs, and we discovered that not one of these properties was a deal. He would lose money on all of them. Auctions are not like writing offers through a realtor for properties listed on the MLS. You have to understand what you are getting into. Luckily, we were able to get the majority of his EMDs returned; otherwise, this would have been his most expensive lesson ever.

Every day in every major metro area there are online auctions and typically at least once a week there are live auctions. Every auction is different and you want to know what the rules are prior to bidding. Some auctions require you have the funds with you to even bid, others will let you bid and give you 10 or 20 days to close. Most auctions have additional fees attached. Some can be as high as 10%

on top of your winning bid. If the maximum price you can pay for a house is $200,000, and the auction has a 5% buyer's premium, you have to stop bidding at $190,000. At $190,000, the 5% buyer's premium equates to an additional $9,500 for a total purchase price of $199,500. Another issue that arises with auctions is you are not always buying properties with clear titles, meaning there could be additional monies owed, additional liens on the property that you will be responsible for. Auctions are not typically for the novice investor. However, most real estate auctions will pay commissions to realtors. If you do want to search the auctions for properties, find a realtor with experience in auctions to guide you through the process.

There are all different ways to get properties. I still buy properties directly from homeowners. I still see "for sale by owner" (FSBO for short) signs in the front yards of homes the owners are trying to sell themselves. When you see one of these, pull over, take a picture of the house and the sign, and give the owners a call. Ask them questions about the house: How big is it? What kind of condition is it in? How many bedrooms does it have? No matter what the answer to your question is, your response is "The house sounds perfect." Ask them how much they want for the house and then let them know you are going to do a little research and call them back to see if it will work for you (I usually tell them I'll drive my wife by it in the evening and if she likes the area, I'll be in touch). These FSBOs are being marketed and sold without realtors, so you need to be prepared to have your own purchase agreement and to make the offer the first time you walk in the door. Over the past 5 years more online resources have been created where homeowners can offer their properties for sale without realtors. So instead of driving up and down every street in town, you can find many of these FSBOs online. These sites let the sellers know they can sell their own houses with ease and skip the 6% realtor commissions and the long drawn-out marketing process. No matter which way you find a FSBO, it's always best to have your repairs estimated and your ARV established beforehand. Put this book down right now, go online, and look up "for sale by owner [your city]." You will find a number of websites that offer listing services for home sellers and home buyers. These are free resources for leads. Typically, if the house is in good shape and there are nice photographs showcasing it, the owners aren't interested in selling fast and low; however, if you find a house with minimal photographs or that looks run-down, go after it. Send the address to your realtor, estimate your repairs, get your ARV, and determine a possible offer price!

The more you network, the more opportunities you will have to find properties. I have had my title/escrow agents send me leads, I had a parent at a soccer game approach me, I've had deals brought to me by my hard money lenders. The more people you know and the more people who know what you are doing, the more opportunities you will be given! When I increased my network both locally and nationally, my business exploded, and I went from doing one deal every 2 months (three or four at a time) to doing upward of five to ten deals per month (twenty to thirty at a time)! We'll do an entire segment on just networking, as it is that powerful.

Your goal is to have an inbox overflowing with potential deals. I review ten to twenty deals a day, eighty to one hundred deals a week, three hundred to four hundred deals a month. If your inbox is not full of deals, you need to do more networking. The key to having an overflowing inbox is making offers. If you get deals but never make offers, the people sending you the deals will stop contacting you. If your inbox is full, do your research and make your offers. If you run out of deals to make offers on, get back to networking! And do not expect good deals to last long, you need to be ready to go. If you have trained your realtors right on how to pull comparables for you, they should be sending you comparables with any deal they send you.

CHAPTER 4 FLIP TIPS

1. Connect with more realtors—most deals come from the MLS.

2. Place your fishing lines with auto searches: the Dirty Dozen, REO properties, dollars per square foot neighborhood searches

3. Buy anything that you can make money on, don't restrict your earning potential.

4. Wholesalers—don't trust their ARV, their repair estimates, or even the addresses they supply. All you need from them is the address, *my* price, and pictures if they have them.

5. Auctions—know the rules before you bid

6. FSBOs are free leads to pursue.

7. The more connections you have, the more deals you will see.

8. You have to make offers to keep your inbox full.

Chapter 5 –

The Conversation, Making the Offer

It's time to pull the trigger! You've found the deal, you've ran your numbers, now you have to make your offer. This is both a scary and an exhilarating process for the first-time investor (and even for seasoned investors). You feel like you are now on the hook for the offer price, whether it be $50,000 or $500,000. Where are you going to get the money? What if they say "yes"? What if they say "no"? What if they laugh at you? Slow down and breathe. Don't worry about all of those what-ifs and just take this one step at a time. You have to think of an offer as the start of a conversation, and this conversation continues all the way until you close on the deal or you or the seller backs out. Your offer is the "hello" that starts the conversation. As we already discussed, most flips are properties that came out of the MLS so your offer, your "hello," will typically be written up on a realtor-approved residential purchase agreement (RPA). It's a good idea to get a blank copy of the RPA from a realtor in each market area in which you are working. Read it and get a good understanding of it. If there are sections you don't understand, ask your realtor to clarify them. It's best to do this right away, that way it doesn't hold you up when you are ready to make offers.

There are going to be some basic items your realtor will need from you to make an offer:

1. Property address

2. Purchase price

3. Buyer name

4. Earnest money deposit

5. Due diligence time frame

6. Closing time frame

7. Contingencies (appraisal, loan, inspections, etc.)

8. Purchasing type (cash or loan)

9. Proof of funds

Let's dig into each one in detail.

1. **Property address:** This one is pretty straightforward. When you email your realtor that you want to make an offer on a property, you'll want to tell him or her which property it is, as you probably have received multiple deals. I like to make sure it's in the subject line of my email as well as it helps keep your emails organized.

2. **Purchase price:** If you ran your numbers correctly, starting at your ARV and working your way down and taking out all of your costs and desired profit, you will come up with your *maximum* purchase price. When I am making

an offer, if my maximum purchase price is $234,000, I might offer $230,000. This gives me some wiggle room if the seller comes back to negotiate. However, in hot markets, where a good deal will be receiving multiple offers, I typically give my best price the first time, as I will have a higher chance of getting my offer accepted.

3. **Buyer name:** I buy my properties in the name of a limited liability corporation, an LLC. I do not buy in my personal name. This is to protect me, my LLC, and my business/funding partners. Some investors purchase using land trusts, others use an S-Corp, some use Series LLCs, these are all different types of *entities*. You will want to consult a real estate attorney and a certified public accountant (CPA) concerning the best way to protect yourself and your assets and to give yourself the best tax advantage. Each state is different as to how it sets up and protects businesses; the majority of real estate–based LLCs and corporations are based out of Nevada, Delaware, or Wyoming. I recommend paying a professional to set this up for you. Depending on your circumstances and comfort level, it might be best to have that person also be what is called a resident agent. When you set this up, ask your professional what he or she recommends for you. Make sure it is done right the first time, so you have maximum protection. This process can typically take between 1 and 4 weeks and costs a few thousand dollars, so get this started as soon as you can. However, don't make this a reason to wait on making offers. When I first started out, I bought and sold properties in my own name, because I just didn't know better. Nothing bad happened to me. That being said, I still recommend you get an entity to maximize your protection and tax savings. I buy my flips in the

name of an LLC with an S-Corp designation, because this is the way my CPA said works best for my tax situation. Confused yet? This little piece here on entities and asset protection is just the tip of the iceberg, as these subjects have hundreds of books written about them. I use professionals and experts in these fields for my business and I recommend you do the same.

4. **Earnest money deposit:** An earnest money deposit, or EMD for short, is your sign of good faith that you can and will close on the transaction. Most MLS systems now state how much EMD the seller is requesting. When I make my offers, I like to offer more than they are requesting, which makes my offer look stronger. If the seller posted an EMD of $2,500, I offer $5,000. I personally like increments of $5,000, as it is a strong solid number in my opinion and it has lead to good results in offers getting accepted. The EMD, if the offer is accepted, typically has to be given to a third party within 2 days of the contract being signed by both parties. That third party is typically a title/escrow company or a real estate attorney or the money is placed into the realtor's escrow account. It is not handed to the seller. That way, if you decide to back out of the contract during your due diligence (or for some reason the seller is unable to sell), you are able to get your EMD released back to you in a timely manner. A lot of gurus teach you that you should send a copy of a check with your offer and always offer $10,000 EMD. They suggest a copy of a check so you can just reuse that same copy for every offer. I haven't found any reason to do this, especially in our current world of Internet banking. Most title/escrow companies will not even take a personal or business check anymore. (So why do the gurus still teach this?)

I always send EMDs by wire transfer. It's less work than a check, it's accepted as a normal course of business, it gives you more control as to when you send it, and most importantly, it is readily available funds. This means that if you back out, whoever is holding your money will typically send a wire back to your account instead of having their corporate office mail you a check in 2 to 3 weeks. Keep control of your money.

5. **Due diligence time frame:** Your due diligence time frame is the amount of time you have once the contract is accepted by the seller (and you have been notified in writing of it—an important little legal aspect) to do your inspections, get quotes from your contractor, get insurance quotes, and so on. Basically, this is the time you have to decide whether you are going to move forward with this deal. I generally ask for 10 days of due diligence on my offers. The smaller the number of days you ask for, the stronger the offer. However, you want to make sure you give yourself enough time to actually complete your due diligence. Do not squander this time. Here are the answers you need to get while completing your due diligence:

    a. Confirm the ARV with your realtor *and* two other realtors. Remember, this is the most important number of your deal, and you want to make sure it is right. I have all three realtors tell me what they think the ARV is, and then I also have them send me the comparables (based on my criteria) they used to determine it; that way I have the data to review and can come up with my own ARV.

b. Get three contractor bids, written and in hand. We'll discuss contractors in chapter 7, but I always get a minimum of three bids on my properties.

c. Determine how you are going to fund the deal, get three quotes on hard money loans, and contact your private investors. We will discuss funding the deal and HMLs in chapter 6. Just know that you want to have your funding plan secured before the end of your due diligence time period.

d. Walk the property and get pictures. This is when you or your agent and boots on the ground should actually go out and walk the property. Make sure to get plenty of pictures, so you have a great resource to reach back to. I get pictures of the following at a minimum:

1) Two pictures of each side of the exterior of the house from different angles

2) Four roof pictures: two of the front and two of the rear

3) Two pictures of the front yard

4) Two pictures of the rear yard

5) Two pictures of each interior room, opposite corners of the room (this allows you to get counts on doors, windows, fixtures, etc.)

6) One picture under *each* sink. This is a spot where damage can add up due to water damage and water intrusion. Don't forget these.

7) Two to three pictures of visible damage from different angles. Such items as water spots on the ceilings, holes in drywall, damaged carpet, and so on. In some cases you will want to include a reference object so you know the scale of the damage. I will typically use a pen in the photo, and that will help me determine the actual size of the damaged area.

8) Pictures of all mechanical components: heating and cooling units, water heater, appliances, water/gas hook-ups, and so on.

9) A picture of the electric panel (make sure you actually open the cover and take a picture of the breakers/fuses).

10) Pictures of any possible value-added or value-negative items such as views, busy streets, ugly houses across the street, and so on.

If you do your pictures right, you should have around one hundred pictures for one house. This is one of the reasons why I love Dropbox.com. I, or my realtor, can upload these pictures into a folder in Dropbox and then just share that folder. It's a nice and easy process, and so much better than sending pictures via text or email. Pixels are free. You really can't have too many pictures. After you leave the property, you will have questions, and those pictures should have the answers. Taking additional pictures of the property can save you a trip back to the property. Work smarter, not harder.

e. Get three quotes on property insurance: You are going to want to get property insurance. I typically use the bigger insurance companies on my projects, as I want to make sure they are going to pay out if there is a problem. You will want a builder's risk/vacant policy. Different insurance companies and different regions may call the policy by different names. All you have to do when you are getting your quote is tell the agent: I am buying a house which is a fixer-upper, I am going to do repairs to it to make it livable and beautiful, and it will be vacant, can you give me a quote on that? They will know the product you are looking for. Additionally, once they research the property, they will also know if you require such items as flood, hurricane, and/or earthquake insurance. If you are getting a loan on the property, you will need the required insurance. If you are not getting a loan, it will typically be your choice if you want the extra insurance or not. I recommend you get it, because you are better safe than sorry.

The completion of your due diligence is extremely important, as this is the time period you have to decide if you are going to move forward with the deal or back out of the contract. As stated before, you want to get a copy of the RPA, read it, and understand it. There will typically be three or four ways for you to back out of a contract. These "outs" are ways you can legally get out of a contract if you have done everything you were supposed to and within the time frame allotted. Know these. If you back out of the contract *after* your due diligence time period is up, you risk losing your EMD. This is not something that you want to happen. Once I get an offer accepted, I will email my realtor and ask him or her to send me the calculated date and time that my due diligence ends. I want this in writing from them so I know exactly what my time frames are. In some hyper markets you will see buyers placing offers with *zero* days of due diligence. I do not recommend this, as it limits your ability to recoup your EMD if you can't close for some reason. However, if you are able to complete all of your due diligence prior to contract acceptance, that can still work. You just have to be extremely confident in your numbers, most notably the ARV and rehab amounts. Many times with wholesale transactions you will not be allowed a due diligence time frame; that is why it is important that you have a good contractor you trust to walk the property with you when you are viewing properties from a wholesaler. Remember, this is a conversation. If you find something you don't like during your due diligence, instead of backing out of the deal, you can always renegotiate. I will ask for a lower price if my repair estimate was off. You won't get it if you don't ask for it. Just make sure to ask for it prior to the end of your due diligence.

6. **Closing time frame:** In contracts, this is typically referred to as the "close of escrow," or COE for short. I will generally make my offers with a 20-day closing time. A standard financed offer by Joe and Jane Homebuyer will have a closing time frame between 30 and 45 days and will have multiple contingencies attached (subject to the sale of their house, subject to loan approval, subject to appraised value, etc.). A 20-day closing time frame should be strong enough for the seller to be excited about your offer *and* give you the time you need to complete your due diligence, determine your ARV, get your rehab numbers from your contractor, and line up the funding of the project.

7. **Contingencies:** Contingencies are normal items in a contract that mean item ABC has to happen for item XYZ to happen. In standard retail contracts this is best

exemplified when Joe and Jane Homebuyer say they will buy a house but it is contingent on them receiving a loan on the property. When I make my offers, I have my agents write into the offer "This offer is *not* contingent on appraisal or loan approval." In the eyes of a standard seller, this makes your offer stronger. Let's take it a step further and ask the question: What are you giving up by saying this? Nothing. Have I told you to get an appraisal on your properties? No. Additionally, your offer price, if they accept, will be below what an appraisal would come in at anyway. This is a way to make your offer look stronger without giving them anything else.

8. **Purchasing type (cash or loan):** I always make my offers as cash offers, even if I am planning on getting a hard money loan. You may come across realtors and buyers who cry and complain that you said it was a cash deal, but now you are getting a loan. I tell them "Who cares? You are still getting all of your money and it changes nothing on your end. My lender can close on or prior to the closing date." I have never had a seller back out of a deal because I changed to financing from cash. Yes, it is a little bit of a bait and switch, but it only costs you money, not them. Most real estate investors have the mindset that hard money loans are the same as a cash purchase—it's just not their cash.

9. **Proof of funds:** A proof of funds, or POF for short, is a document that shows you have the money available to buy the property. This is typically a bank statement or a letter from your financial agent stating you have more money than the offer price. For instance, if you are making a cash offer of $128,000 for a property, you will want to show a

bank statement with more than $128,000 in it. What do you do if you don't have the $128,000? Don't worry. This POF does not necessarily have to be in your entity name. If you have financial partners willing to finance your flips, get a copy of their POF and have them write a letter stating that you have access to their funds for the purpose of the purchase of the property. This will typically suffice for most sellers. Additionally, some hard money lenders will also provide financing approval letters for you to use. Just remember, cash is king, and if you can show that you have access to actual cash, whether it be your cash or a partner's cash, it is stronger than any letter from a financing institution.

Once you give your realtor the nine items listed above, he or she will input this information into the RPA and then the realtor should send the contract to you in an online platform for electronic initials and signatures such as DocuSign or Authentisign. If the realtor wants to meet you somewhere and get "wet" signatures (where you actually put a real pen to real paper), tell him or her to get with the times and send it electronically. You don't want to be late in getting your offer to a listing realtor because your realtor had to drive across town to meet you the next day after dropping the kids off at school. Once you have made a decision to submit an offer, you want that offer to be put in the hands of the seller as quickly as possible. It is important that you read and know what it is you are signing. Don't assume the realtor will fill out the RPA correctly. Make sure he or she put your numbers into the contract; you have to become the expert. Sometimes realtors will throw extra forms onto the RPA, such as a brokerage fee agreement where they try to get an extra $300–800 commission from you. Or maybe they include an exclusive agency

agreement with the RPA, which states you will buy all your properties from them, and if you buy any property (even if it is from a
wholesaler or a homeowner), you still owe them commission. Make
sure to read what you are signing! If you don't understand a form
that was sent to you, contact the person who sent it. This holds true
for any form, whether it be from a realtor, hard money lender, escrow
coordinator, or someone else. Make sure you understand what you
are signing. It is okay to ask questions! Additionally, some realtors
love to include additional forms that are not required but are there
to cover and protect them. If it's not required, don't sign it, you need
to worry about you!

Once you have signed the RPA, your realtor will email it to the
seller's realtor, who will present it to the seller, and the conversation
has begun. Now it's time for the seller to decide whether to answer
back. The seller's answer will typically fall into one of three categories:

1. Offer accepted—Congratulations! The seller accepted your
    offer as it was presented and now it's time to start your due
    diligence.

2. Counteroffer—This means the seller didn't like some
    aspect of your offer. It could range from the price to the
    closing date to the escrow office. Read over the coun-
    teroffer, rerun your numbers, and see if it still works.
    Remember, you can always make a counter-counteroffer.
    It is just a conversation. There is usually some give and
    take in a contract negotiation. Do not get emotional, stick
    to your numbers, and make sure the deal works for you.

3. Rejected—The seller may just flat out reject your offer.
    A seller may do this in writing, via a phone call from
    their realtor, or by just ignoring you completely and not

responding. If the seller sends me a rejection in writing or verbally, I will have my realtor follow up in 2 weeks to see whether the current buyer is performing. If the current buyer isn't performing and the seller thinks the deal might be falling out of contract, my realtor than asks to submit our offer as a backup offer. If we don't receive any response from the seller's side, I have my realtor follow up in 2 days to find out the status.

In this business, one offer is not enough. It's exciting to make that offer, you've taken the plunge into the world of real estate investing, now it's time to make more! Any given week I make between ten and thirty offers. I am not a fan of lowball offers. A lowball offer is an offer at $33,000 when the property is listed at $120,000. Is that seller even going to consider that offer? Most likely not, and you have just wasted your time and your realtor's time. If you continue to insist on lowball offers, you run the risk of losing your realtors, as they won't take you seriously and will see you as a time drain instead of a potential paycheck. I see some investors who send out hundreds of these offers every week just hoping to get one or two. It is not a method I am fond of (I even get offers on my remodeled properties from investors like this!). I want you to make researched and informed offers on properties that people actually want to sell. When you are first starting out, you should shoot for one offer per day (another reason why it is good to have multiple realtors working for you). If you make thirty offers at $100,000 in 1 month, does that mean you are on the hook for $3,000,000? No, even if all offers are accepted, you still are not on the hook for all of that money. If you get multiple offers accepted, you better get cranking on your due diligence items! Pick out the best deals and proceed with those. If you get more deals than you can handle, you can always try to wholesale those deals to other investors too! The quicker you can make researched and informed offers, the more deals you will get. To get offers accepted, you have to make offers.

Prior to closing on your property, there are going to be some important items you will want to make sure happen. The title/escrow company and the realtors involved will all be babysitting the deal to make sure it closes and everything goes smoothly. Remember, the realtors and the title/escrow company only get paid when the property closes; they have a vested interest in this deal. You, however, will need to be in contact with your money person, whether it be a hard money lender or a private investor, during the closing process. If you are getting a hard money loan, the HML will request the contact information for the title/escrow company so they can make sure all of their paperwork is set. If you are dealing with a private investor, you will be handling your own paperwork. I typically have my private investors wire their funds to the title/escrow company one day before closing just to be safe. Prior to closing the deal, you will also want to pick which contractor you are going to use and find out when he or she can get started. Ideally, your contractor can get started the day after closing. Remember, the longer you have the property, the less money you are going to make. You want your projects to move. For the contractor to get started, he or she will typically need the utilities turned on. After I have made the decision that I am purchasing the property, I will schedule my utilities to be turned on the day after closing. Some utility companies can take 1 or 2 weeks to schedule service. Most realtors will be able to get you the contact information for the local utility companies.

One of the most important preclosing items you will need to do is a final walkthrough. Prior to closing, you or your representative will need to go back to the property and make sure it is in the same condition it was in when you first looked at it. How much can change in a couple weeks? A lot. If it was a vacant property, you may find that the property now has squatters or has been vandalized. If it was a property with occupants, and they were supposed to move out, you may find them still living there. I recently had a property I was supposed to close on a Friday afternoon. That Thursday night the owner was using the barbecue and burned down a portion of the house and the garage. The fire department estimated the damage at $65,000. The garage was a complete loss, the property now needed a new roof, and the exterior was burned and damaged. The house was definitely not in the same condition it was when I agreed to pay for it. In these instances, you typically have three options, but make sure to read your contract to know what your rights are. Option 1: Close on the property and just deal with the problem yourself. I'll do this if it is a minor item, and I know I won't get anything from the other side. I've had owners take all of the appliances out of the property when the contract stated they were going to leave the appliances. I could have sold those appliances and made a few hundred dollars, but I didn't need them for the property, as I was going to install new appliances anyway. Option 2: Delay the closing until the seller rectifies the problem. In my fire-damaged property, the seller still wanted me to close at the same price; his reasoning was that the roof wasn't in great shape anyway. I told the seller that I would keep the price the same if he fixed everything. He didn't want to fix anything, so we went to the next option. Option 3: Renegotiate the price. There is always a price you can associate with damage. In my fire-damaged property I asked for a $35,000 price reduction. The seller didn't have insurance, otherwise I would have asked for the insurance proceeds to be paid directly to me. You sometimes have to be creative in this option, and it helps if you really know what the seller's motivation is. No matter what option you go with, you have to stick with your numbers. If the property is still a deal, don't let your, or the seller's, pride get in the way of you making money. Always make sure you do a final walkthrough on a property, because once you buy it, it's yours.

CHAPTER 5 FLIP TIPS

1. An offer is the start of a conversation.

2. If you don't make offers, you won't get any deals.

3. Know your dates. Once an offer is accepted, bring up your calendar and get moving!

4. Due diligence is the key, whether it is prior to or after the offer is accepted, the clock is ticking, and you need to verify your numbers.

5. If you don't ask for it, you won't get it. Every part of a contract can be negotiated, from price to time frame to title companies.

6. Don't be emotional, stick with your numbers. If the deal doesn't work, and you can't get a price reduction, move on to the next one.

7. Preclosing items are a must: money, utilities, and the final walkthrough.

8. Schedule your utilities and contractor for the day after closing. Every day the house sits is money out of your pocket.

CHAPTER 6 –

How to Fund the Deal

The question. When that guru was on stage, I asked "Where do you find good hard money lenders?" I had already been working with a couple of local HMLs, but I wanted to find out how to get better rates. The guru's response as he sat on a stool in front of these 500 paying attendees? He looked away from me and smirked at the other side of the audience and did a little head roll and responded, "There's this little thing called Google." If someone paid you $40,000, would you treat them that way? I wouldn't. He was right, though. They are on Google, you just need to understand how they work, what questions to ask, and how they are limited. All things that were not explained in the seminar. If you have your own money to fund your real estate endeavors, great for you! Get after it. However, it will run out, as you can only do so many projects with your own money. If you only have a couple of dimes to rub together, you will need help with money to fund deals. Hard money lenders, or HMLs, are the key to this business, and you will have to use them.

Many investors have a hard time swallowing the hard money interest rates, which can range from 8% up to 18%. The first deal I received a hard money loan on I was charged 3.5 points (1 point is 1% of the loan amount) and 14% interest. Crazy? The house was a wreck and needed more than $40,000 in repairs; no traditional lender would have lent on the house. At the time I was transitioning from being a self-employed appraiser to a full-time real estate investor with sporadic income streams—not the best candidate for a home loan from a traditional lender. Hard money lenders look past all of that. Where a traditional bank or mortgage company views your relationship as a long-term commitment in which you are the most important part of it, hard money lenders look at the deal first, because they know they are only going to be with you for a short-term period, typically somewhere between 6 and 12 months. A traditional lender lends on you; a hard money lender lends on the property. If it is a good deal, there is a lender out there for it.

So where do you find hard money lenders? Google of course! Go to Google, or any search engine you prefer, and type in "Hard money lenders [your city]." In this search you will get a mixed list full of real hard money lenders who will lend directly to you and hard money brokers. A hard money broker is a company or an individual who will take your deal and shop it around to actual hard money lenders. The more generic the name, the more likely it isn't a direct lender. A hard money broker will try to make a lot of money off you, but typically can't perform or perform on time. Wouldn't you rather go directly to the *real* lenders? These are signs that a company may be a broker, it will have a generic company name like CaliforniaHardMoneyloansnow.com. Real companies have names like Weber Lending or Midtown Mortgage and should be able to give you a tight range, 11–12% or 2–3 points. A hard money broker will typically answer with a wide range, something like 10–16% or 2–6 points. If you get a wide-range answer, stay away.

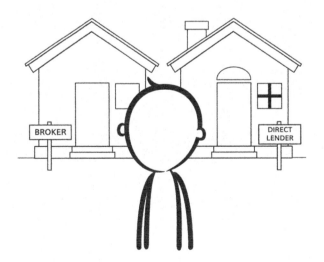

Here are some more tips to determine whether a company is a hard money broker and you should move on:

- If it advertises it gives loans in all fifty states, it is probably a broker. Real HMLs typically only cover their states and a few other adjacent states, but not all 50.

- If the email ends in @gmail.com, @yahoo.com, or some other generic dot-com address, it is most likely an independent broker and you should stay away. Real companies have real emails.

- If it advertises it gives loans from $10,000 to $100,000,000, it is not real. Trust me on this, if you are a company that is closing loans in the $100,000,000 range, you will not even consider doing a loan for $10,000, because that number is outside your business model.

- If it requests money upfront for items like application fees, credit reports, or deal analyses, it is typically a broker and generates its money on these bogus upfront costs. I have never paid for these and you shouldn't either. The only item I have ever paid for out of pocket prior to the loan closing is an appraisal, which some HMLs may require as a prior-to-funding condition.

HMLs will work with you! Remember, a real HML is going to be helpful—it only gets paid when it gives you a loan! If an HML tells you it thinks your ARV is wrong, it isn't doing it because it doesn't like you. It is protecting its investors and their loans. An HML gets the money it lends from its own private pool of investors and sometimes from large-fund credit lines. The rates an HML pays its investors are typically in the 8–10% range. The HML will then make its profit by charging you a slightly higher percentage rate and points. You can typically find an investor advertising page for most HMLs on their websites where they state how much they pay their investors. If they offer their investors a 10% return, they won't be able to give you a rate less than 10% on your loan, so don't expect it. Knowing that an HML has to pay its investors should let you know that there is a limit on how low its costs can go. Additionally, the fact that a HML has investors it is answerable to is the very reason why it only wants to lend on good deals. If an HML tells you your ARV is wrong, ask why it thinks that. You don't want to get into a bad deal either. The HML is another set of eyes on your project, which I consider a good thing.

If you can get a recommendation from another investor who has used an HML before, that is always preferable. You want to make sure the HML will actually perform, meaning it will show up to the closing table with the money as promised. Even though a new HML you found online answered all your questions correctly and sounded legitimate, it can still flake when it comes to closing, and you are in a bad position at the closing table. Ask around at your local meet-up groups or on Facebook group pages for recommendations. If someone does give a recommendation, ask how many deals he or she has done with the HML and whether there is anything you need to watch out for.

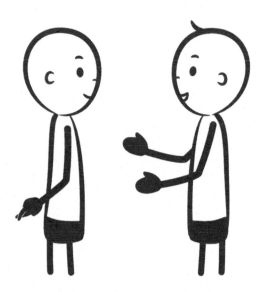

The more information you have, the better. If someone does not give the recommendation publicly and tries to hold it as a secret, he or she is probably going to get a kickback because he or she is just a private hard money broker. There are people who make their money this way; that is why it is important to ask follow-up questions.

Most HMLs want you to have some skin in the game, some money out of your own pocket invested into the deal. A hard money loan will typically be based on one of the three following models:

- Hard money loan based on purchase price: Depending on your deal and your experience, some HMLs will give a loan to value (LTV) in the range of 65–100% of your purchase price. In this case, the "value" is determined by the purchase price and not the actual market value. If you have a purchase price of $140,000, and the HML tells you it will give you a loan at 70%, it will give you a loan of $98,000 ($140,000 × 0.70). As you do more loans with a company like this, it will typically increase the LTV it lends on. I have companies that will lend me 100% of my purchase price.

- Hard money loan based on purchase price and repairs: Depending on your deal, a hard money lender may offer to fund your repairs as well. If your project has a purchase price of $140,000 and $40,000 in repairs, and the HML tells you it will give you a loan at 70% on the purchase price and 90% of the repairs, it will give you a loan of $134,000 ($140,000 × 0.70 = $98,000 + $40,000 × 0.90 = $36,000). The repair funds are not typically given upfront; they are given out in draws. To receive a repair draw, you will typically be required to provide evidence of work having been completed equal to the amount of the repair requested. If you have finished $10,000 of repairs on the property, the lender will typically then release $10,000 in a repair draw to you. You really need to pay attention to your cash flow, as you are fronting the money for the repairs, and the hard money lender is only providing funds after portions of the work have been completed.

- Hard money loan based on ARV: Some HMLs lend based on ARV. This will typically be in the range of 60–75% of the ARV. If your same $140,000 + $40,000 project has an ARV of $250,000, and the HML tells you it will lend on 70% of ARV, that means it will give you a loan amount *up to* $175,000. *However*, it will typically not give you more than the project is worth and will require you to have at least 10% skin in the game, or in this case, 10% of the project cost, or $18,000 ($180,000 × 0.10). If you subtract $18,000 from the total project costs of $180,000, that gives you a maximum loan amount of $162,000.

Each of these scenarios can work well for different projects and will also vary based on your personal financial position. Even if I have plenty of money in my own accounts, I still tell the HML that I want as much money as it will give me. When I am interviewing an HML, here are the eight main questions I ask:

1. What is your interest rate?

2. How many points do you charge?

3. What is the loan to value (LTV) you typically lend at?

4. Is your LTV based on purchase price or ARV?

5. Do you lend on repairs?

6. How quickly can you close?

7. Does your company charge any additional fees?

8. How many deals do I have to do before I get your best rates?

I do not let the HML get off the phone until I have the answers to these eight questions. Good HML rates are in the 10–12% range and points should be in the 2- to 4-point range. The starting LTV should at least be in the 70–80% range of purchase price, and if it offers repairs, 80–100% of repairs. If you aren't getting these numbers or better, keep searching, keep calling.

HMLs are not your only source for funding. There is money all around you. Let your network know you need money! If you don't put it out there, you won't find it. I have raised money from many different sources over the years—family members, my realtors/contractors, private investors, other people I met at seminars, and more.

They are out there! The first million-dollar investor I convinced to work with me found me from an ad I posted on Craigslist! I posted the ad in several cities in California and on the East Coast and it read:

Great Returns Available In Real Estate, Seasoned Investor Looking for Money Partners

I am a successful real estate investor experienced in fixing and flipping residential real estate. I have more deals than I have money right now, so I have an opening for another money partner. I do the work, you bring in the money (secured in 1st position by the real estate), and we split the profits. Serious investors only. Contact me for more details. Send your full contact information and I will reply.

The investor replied to this ad and asked a bunch of questions; we went back and forth for a couple of months and then silence. I wrote him off as a guy who was just after my knowledge. About 9 months after the initial contact he called me up and said he was now ready to invest. I said great and started putting him on deals. This was during the real growth of my business, and I only had so much of my own money. To do more deals, I needed more cash. To get more cash I had to give up bigger chunks of the profit. With this investor I did what are called 50/50s or joint ventures or property partnerships. The basic premise is that the investor comes in with all of the money—the purchase price, closing costs, repairs, and carrying costs; I do all of the work; and the end profit gets split at closing with each side getting 50% of the net profit. If you have ever heard a radio ad or infomercial for a real estate seminar that says they are going to teach you how to flip houses with no money out of your pocket, this is the way it's done. These companies try to make it seem like it is a big secret. The fact of the matter is, flipping houses with no money out of your pocket is extremely difficult. Before you can even get this investor to say "yes" to a deal, you need to have that deal under your control, locked up, under contract. If you have a property under contract, that means you have had to put in your EMD, which is money out of your own pocket. There are people out there who will lend you the money for EMD, but they charge you for it and at rates typically higher than the HML rates we already discussed. Yes, the investor who comes in can reimburse you for your EMD so that it can go back into your pocket. What I am telling you is that if you do not have $5,000 or more in a bank account, it is going to be very hard for you to get this business running without some type of partner. If you are not saving money, you better start. A lot of investors you meet will want you to have some skin in the game too, even if it is only the EMD. Be prepared for that.

Once you have found people willing to invest with you, what's next? As soon as one of my investors agrees to fund a deal, I send him or her a contract explaining the terms of our deal and what is expected of both partners. We both sign the contract, I have the title/escrow company (or an attorney) create a note and deed of trust, and this is recorded against the property. This is essentially the same type of paperwork a major bank will place on a property when you get a home loan. The property cannot be sold without this lien being paid off. This paperwork will typically cost a few hundred dollars and should be included in the overall cost of the deal, meaning the expense is shared by you and the investor. This is the warm and fuzzy protection that you offer your investors to make them feel good about investing with you. I have my investors wire their money directly to the title/escrow company when it is time to close the deal. The money does not come directly to my personal or business bank accounts. When the property sells, the title/escrow company wires the initial investment plus the investor's share of profit directly to the investor. You must protect your investors.

When I am seeking investors, I typically tell them, "I want your money, not your mind." What this means is I do not expect them or want them to help in the remodeling and selling of the property. They are investing with me, with you, because we are the experts in our industry. We know what to do and what not do on a project; we are trained professionals. You do not want too many cooks in the kitchen. I typically update my investors four or five times during the project after they have funded it. Here is the typical timeline of those updates:

1. Project is closed and date when rehab will get started.

2. Once rehab is started, I create a shared folder on Dropbox. com (you can use Google Docs or another program for this) and I send the investor a link to the folder. As the project progresses, I continually add photos to this folder, so the investor can look at the progress of the project whenever he or she wants.

3. Once rehab is completed and the project is being placed on market.

4. When a contract is agreed upon and the buyer has put an EMD in. I do not tell my investor about every contract or bother them with showing details unless he or she specifically asks me. My investor should know that I am negotiating the best deal for both of us.

5. Two to three days prior to closing I will notify the investor of the closing date and provide a spreadsheet of expenses

that shows the profit on the project and what his or her share is. The title/escrow company will typically also contact the investor around this time concerning their payoff amount. This is the amount of their investment plus their profit share that you have provided them.

For some investors this is not enough hand-holding, and they will want more. It is for you to decide how much you give them. I tell my investors, "I know you worked hard for your money, now let me make your money work hard for you." You will have investors who want to view the properties during the construction; just make sure they know they are not supposed to show up unannounced. Every investor/lender is different. Some are good and some can be bad. I have had investors who wanted to fund every one of my deals, but I turned them away because they were too difficult to work with. You can be selective in your investors once you have options. If you only have one investor, use him or her, but in this business, you can never stop looking for money and looking for cheaper money. Although I started out giving my investors 50% of the net profits, over time I gave them smaller and smaller percentages. They knew their money was safe with me and I would perform, so they were willing to take less profit with less risk. As I found more investors, I was able to leverage the power of these additional monies. Each new round of investors I went after, I would offer lower splits and percentages than I was currently paying. I would then tell the 50/50 investor that I had an investor willing to take a 40/60 split, and if he wanted to continue to invest, he would have to match it. Eventually I got most of my investors down to just a flat percentage, much like a hard money lender. I still give a select few of my investors 50/50 splits just out of loyalty. Never forget those that helped you get to where you are.

What if you have limited funds and you can't find someone with a couple hundred thousand willing to invest with you? There is another option called gap lending. Gap lending is the combination of a hard money loan along with a private investor. The hard money loan is the bulk of the funds needed to purchase a property, with the HML secured in a first position on the property, meaning the HML gets paid first when the property is sold. The gap lender brings in the rest of the funds for the deal, whatever the HML doesn't provide for the purchase and repairs plus all of the costs for closing and the carrying costs for the property throughout the life of the project (this includes the mortgage payments to the HML, utilities, etc.). This is another big push at real estate seminars, and it can be a win-win scenario for both the flipper and the gap lender. However, there is more risk too. Your carrying costs add up quickly, especially with a hard money loan. If the project goes long and you go over budget on your rehab, you can quickly get into a negative-equity situation, meaning you will lose money on the project. With this greater risk should come greater reward. The reward for the flipper is simply that he or she gets to do a project with no out-of-pocket costs and still gets 50% of the profit. The gap lender, who is in second position and really carries the most risk, gets 50% of the profit as well. Why do they do this? They do this because investors focus on something called the annualized return on investment, or AROI. I am sure you have all heard the myth that if you put your money in the stock market, over the long term you will realize a return of 6–8%. That 6–8% is the AROI on your money. Investors think in yearly terms, not just the length of a single flip property. Using the prior example, ($140,000 purchase price, $40,000 repairs, $250,000 ARV), let's plug that into our profit equation:

$250,000 (ARV)

- $2,800 (purchase closing costs are approx. 2% of purchase price)

- $40,000 (repairs/remodel cost)

- $3,000 (always budget for 6 months of holding costs, $500 × 6)

- $20,000 (8% for sale closing costs to pay realtors and title/escrow)

- $140,000 (purchase price)

  = $44,200 profit

The investor would have to put up the funds for the purchase ($140,000), the repairs ($40,000), the purchase closing costs ($2,800), and the carrying costs ($3,000). The sale closing costs come out of the proceeds and do not come out of pocket. The total out-of-pocket expenses on this deal would be $185,800. The investor would make 50% of the profit, which equates to $22,100. That is a project return on investment (ROI) of 11.9% ($22,100/$185,800 = 0.119) if the project were to go 6 months; annualized, that would be a 23.8% return or 23.8% AROI. Much better than the stock market historical trend of 6–8% we have all been told about. Now let's assume you did get a hard money loan on the project. Again, using the example above, if your project has a purchase price of $140,000 and $40,000 in repairs, and the HML tells you it will give you a loan at 70% on the purchase price and 90% of the repairs, it will give you a loan of $134,000 ($140,000 × 0.70 = $98,000 + $40,000 × 0.90 = $36,000). The equation now looks like this:

$250,000 (ARV)

- $2,800 (purchase closing costs are 2% of purchase price, use the list price to estimate this)

- $40,000 (remodel cost)

- $3,000 (always budget for 6 months of holding costs, $500 × 6)

- $20,000 (8% of ARV for sale closing costs to pay realtors and title/escrow)

- $17,500 (7% of ARV for approx. hard money loan costs)

- $140,000 (purchase price)

  = $26,700 Profit

Why is the profit less? Because you need to calculate in your loan costs. However, your cash out-of-pocket changes as well. Instead of the investor putting in $184,400, he or she only has to come up with $69,300 ($185,800 − $134,000 loan amount + $17,500 in estimated loan costs). The investor would still make 50% of the profit, which equates to $13,350. That is a project ROI of 19.3% if the project were to go 6 months; annualized, that would be a 38.5% return. With more risk, there should be more reward, and that is why there are investors willing to do gap lending. Not only did their amount of return go up, but now the can do more deals as well.

There are all different scenarios that will entice private investors. The main thing is to remember they are typically comparing your offer to what they think they can get on the safe bet of the stock market (which we all know is not as safe as we think it is). When you are talking to investors, talk to them in their language, let them know both the ROI of the project and the AROI. If I were to tell a private lender, "Give me $100,000 and I will give you $3,000 back," he or she would never do that. It sounds too risky. However, if I were to rephrase it and let the lender know that I could "give a 36% AROI on $100,000," he or she would jump at it and ask for more information. I would then explain that I have a real estate investment that is estimated to go 1 month and that he or she could be in a secured first position and would receive $103,000 back at the end of that month. It's all on how you word your proposal and whether you talk in their language.

Don't be pushy either, let investors make up their own minds. Write up a nice presentation on the project and email it to them. The presentation should have six or eight pictures of the property, a brief synopsis on the remodel that you will be completing, the estimated time the project will take, and the estimated profit the project will make. I also include three of the comparable sales that support the ARV in my presentations. I end the presentation with what I want from them and what I will be giving them in return. This would be a calculated breakdown of the project costs, estimated profit, and profit splits with ROI and AROI noted. Additionally, in my presentations I always underpromise so that I can overdeliver. If I think my ARV is $250,000, I may present it with an ARV of $240,000 or $245,000. This gives me a little cushion in my numbers. If you exceed your investor's expectations on a deal, he or she is more likely to reinvest with you. However, don't make a bad deal look good by inflating numbers. Changing the ARV from $250,000 up to $270,000 to convince an investor to work with you is not a way to do business. Only get into deals where the numbers truly work. A good presentation is typically the difference between getting an investor to work with you or not work with you. Don't just stop at one investor, you will need more. As you get into bigger projects and multiple projects, you will tap out the pockets of your investors (before they are refilled when the projects sell of course). Along with constantly looking for properties, you should constantly be looking for money. Once you find the money, make sure you are putting it all to work. If you let your investors' money sit, they will find another home for it.

CHAPTER 6 FLIP TIPS

1. Direct hard money lenders are better than brokers.

2. Interview HML, get all of your questions answered.

3. Never stop looking for money, never stop looking for cheaper money.

4. Keep looking for money partners—the more money you have, the more deals you can do.

5. $100,000 to make $3,000 *or* a 36% AROI. Talk in their language

6. A good presentation is key to convincing people to work with you. Underpromise, overdeliver.

7. Always keep the money working.

CHAPTER 7 –

Finding, Managing, and Paying Contractors

Finding a good contractor who has fair pricing and does high-quality work is one of the hardest things in this business. It doesn't matter if you are a seasoned professional or you are just starting out, this process never really changes. It comes down to this: you have to have contractors and handymen on your team, and you need them but they don't always think they need you. The reason why you need them is pretty simple; they are going to do the remodel for you. Your time is more valuable finding the deals, networking, building your team, finding money, and running your numbers. You should not be lifting a hammer or a paintbrush. If you want to do that, you might as well just get a second job working for a construction company, as you will typically make more doing that. If you are the one lifting the hammers and brushes, your project will suffer. Even if you are an experienced contractor, it will go more slowly and keep your business from growing. You must hire out the work. Why do contractors need you? Contractors need you because you have the ability to offer them repeated work. They don't have to run around giving a bunch of quotes and dealing with homeowners living in houses. Your projects are vacant and ready to go. Nice and easy. This is the type of work the contractors should love.

They don't have to work around the schedule of the homeowner's children eating breakfast or a homeowner who can't make up his or her mind and keeps changing and delaying a small project. A typical project from a homeowner might be in the range of $3,000 to $6,000, but a typical project from a real estate investor like you will be in the $30,000 range. Don't you think a contractor would like to do one project versus five or ten to make his or her profit? Some contractors will view it this way; others won't. You have to sell yourself to them, give them your real estate story. Let them know what your future together holds.

You will want to get your rehab quotes during your due diligence period. This means prior to buying the property. You don't want to buy a property, get rehab numbers, and find out your estimated numbers were wrong and you are going to lose money! As you start your real estate–investing business you need to be looking for three things: properties, money, and contractors. You never stop looking for these, and they are all equally important. I have known new investors who only focused on getting a deal lined up. Once they had the deal under contract, they started looking for contractors and money. Guess what? Their due diligence time was wasted, and they couldn't close the deal and lost it. As soon as you get the property under contract you want to start contacting your contractors for quotes and letting your money people know they are needed. To do this, you need to already have the contractors vetted and ready to give you quotes. There needs to be an existing understanding between the two of you. So where do you find contractors? Everywhere and anywhere. Here is a list of places I have found contractors in the past:

1. Thumbtack.com

2. AngiesList.com

3. Craigslist.com

4. Referrals from Facebook friends

5. Referrals from Facebook groups

6. Home Depot or Lowes contractor desks

7. Local real estate–investing clubs

8. Meetup.com real estate–investing groups

9. Yellow pages (yes, they still exist)

10. Posting fliers on dumpsters in front of other rehab projects

11. Calling realtors of the comparable sales for contractor referrals

Thumbtack.com is a great resource and has contractors and handymen in most major markets. I want you to go to Thumbtack. com right now and place an ad for a contractor. It's a simple process, and it's okay if you don't have a project ready to go yet. Follow the simple steps on the website. You need "general contracting." You will be asked a series of questions regarding your upcoming projects. You can use your personal home as a reference for answering these questions. As you fill out the forms, remember, you are looking for a general contractor who can handle your project from start to finish and can manage everything from kitchens to bedrooms to bathrooms to garages—a typical major remodel. On Thumbtack.com and most of the other sites like this, you will be asked for a description of your project. My standard description explains who I am, what I am doing (flipping a house), and the basics of what I need. It will read something like this:

> I have a property under contract that I need a contractor to do a full remodel on, kitchen, bathrooms, paint, granite, etc. This is for a flip.

I let them know immediately that this is going to be a flip. Some contractors may only want to work retail jobs, as they think they will get more money doing this. If they know they don't want to work on flips, they won't contact you. By letting them know the purpose of the remodel upfront, you will end up saving time and energy. Sometimes you will be asked to include pictures or addresses on these websites; I leave these blank or just include information from a prior property or a current project I am considering.

The goal of placing this ad is to have general contractors contact you who are interested in more business and understand what it takes to flip a house. These are more fishing lines you are putting out there. The great thing about most of these sites is the contractor will contact you; you are not cold calling them. If they are contacting you, that means they are actively looking for work. Think of these websites as job boards, they are the Internet corkboards where you are posting a job. If contractors are busy and booked out for months, they won't contact you. If they are contacting you, they need work.

If contractors need work, their prices should be more reasonable; if contractors don't need work, they will bid your project high, because it would have to be worth it for them to work the extra hours. As with your realtors, you want to find contractors who are hungry! Beware the contractors who drive big expensive trucks that are always clean and contractors who have flashy websites. If they have these, it typically means they are only looking to bid high-retail quotes and won't work for you on your flip numbers.

When you are first starting out, you are going to have to contact *a lot* of contractors. I have a ten to three rule. What this means is that you will probably have to schedule ten contractors to view a property to get your three quotes. Many contractors are flaky, lazy, busy, or not punctual. Most contractors will actually agree with this. If I am scheduling ten contractors to view a property, this all needs to be done during my due diligence, and this is the typical breakdown:

1. Three contractors do not show up.

2. Two contractors show up and tell you flat out the job is too big or too small for them and they can't do it.

3. Two contractors who show up state they will need to get their subcontractors back out to quote the rest of it.

4. Three contractors out of the seven who actually went to the property send you bids.

You will have to go through this multiple times. It is the nature of the business. Despite all of my success, I still have these issues in markets where I invest. In my active markets, I typically have one or two of my regular contractors quote a property, but I am always looking for new contractors, and it is also a way to keep my current contractors honest. You may have that contractor you know and love and trust; he has done a couple projects for you and maybe he worked on your house and did a good job. But, what if he doesn't have a good roofer and you get overcharged $3,000 for a roof? Or what if you are getting close to the holidays and the contractor is thinking about vacation time and presents for his kids and he bumps his bid an extra

$5,000. Even though I have my regular contractors bid the job, I'll still get bids from new contractors. Always get three bids.

When contractors contact me from one of my ads, or I get a referral from a friend or realtor, I want to get that contractor on the phone to see whether we are a good fit as soon as possible. I want to find out if that contractor can do everything on the project from start to finish. From A to Z. When you ask them these questions, they will typically answer with a "yes." Remember, they are hungry for work. My next question will be: "Is there anything that you can't do or don't do?." Again, they will typically say "yes" to this as well, even though 4 seconds ago they just told me they can do everything. The typical items contractors say they can't or don't do are: roofing, air conditioning, electrical, and landscaping. When they tell me they can't do something, I ask if they have someone they can call who can do it, because "I don't want to have to bring out subcontractors to your project." Notice the use of "your" in my sentence. If you word it like that, it helps them start thinking of the project as theirs already, and they are more apt to show up to quote it and then to provide that written quote. In this phone interview I will reiterate that I flip properties and I am looking for a contractor who can be with me for the long term. I also let them know that I take pride in my projects, and I don't want to put out a cheap or bad product. I let them know I want my projects to be a little better than my competition so my house will sell faster and I can do more deals. Depending on the flow of the conversation, I may also add "I don't pay retail pricing, so if that is all you quote, it's probably best not to waste either of our time. But I also know it needs to be a win-win relationship between us." If they answer the questions correctly, and I have a good feeling from them, I will let them know that I will call them back when I get my next property under contract and have them quote it out. I put them in my database and know I have them waiting for my call.

Once I get a property under contract and I am ready to start sending the contractor out to the property to quote it, if it is a new contractor who hasn't worked for me yet, I will send him or her a link to one of my past projects so he or she can see what type of end product I have in mind. If you haven't done a project, you can send a link to one of the comparables you used to establish your ARV. This way, the contractor has a basic idea of what type of remodel I am looking at doing before he or she views the property. I like to meet the contractor at the property (or I have my local boots on the ground do it, if it is a remote project). It's always best to reconfirm the appointment 2 hours before the scheduled meeting time; typically, 50% of contractors will have forgotten about the meeting, be running late, or thought it was for a different day. I used to not call to confirm and would just wait to see if the contractor would show up, just as a test. However, I found I was wasting my time. I thought I would have an upper hand in negotiations, because the contractors would feel bad for making me wait or having to reschedule. Nope, that didn't work. They were even more prone to not bid the property after that. Come on contractors, don't you realize we are trying to give you money?! You must hold their hands. Call or text to reconfirm your meeting time.

As you walk the property with the contractor, point out the items you want repaired or replaced. Take the lead, but let the contractor talk too. Although you have a vision for the property, the contractor may see things that also need to be done or can't be done. You want your contractor to be able to solve problems. If your contractor walks into the property, no matter what its condition is, and says, "Wow, this thing needs a lot of work," that is contractor speak for "I'm going to try to charge you a lot of money." My follow-up to a contractor who says something like that is "Well, if it is too much for you, I can get somebody else to do it." That usually shuts the contractor down on the spot and indicates you are serious and won't be a pushover. No job should be intimidating to a contractor, and if it is, that are not the contractor for you. Any construction job is just a stepwise procedure; whether it is a simple carpet and paint remodel or a teardown and rebuild, it's all just one step at a time. After you walk the property with the contractor, ask whether he or she has any questions for you or any questions about the materials you are expecting. Make sure you are both on the same page. Depending on the repairs needed, a contractor may need to send some of their subcontractors back to quote items like new plumbing/electric, roofs, or concrete work. Good contractors will know the pricing of their subs and will be able to bid these out themselves. Before the contractor leaves, I ask "When do you think you will have the bid back to me?." Some will say a day; some will say a week. This puts them on the clock, another item they must perform on, just like showing up for the appointment. A good contractor will be able to have that bid back to you within 2 days. Hold them to it. Start emailing and calling as soon as the deadline has passed. Let them know you need the bid.

The same day you walk the property with the contractor, you will want to send an email listing what you want done to the property, basically the scope of work for the project. You should include everything you talked about, because the contractor probably missed or forgot three or four things you pointed out. You will also want to add a caveat at the bottom of the email, reminding the contractor to add to the quote anything they saw that was needed but you may have missed. I typically will include the link to the property I want my remodel to look like in this email again to remind the contractor of what I am looking for.

There are multiple reasons why you should always get three bids. Despite walking the property with the contractor and outlining the scope of the work, you will find that each contractor probably missed something when creating the bid. Once you get the three bids, you will want to compare them to one another, not just for pricing, but for completeness. The lowest bid is not always the best. Many times I have gone with the contract with the middle or highest bid. I want to use the best contractor for the project, but one that is within the budget. I want the bids to be broken up line by line. I don't care if the contractors number out how many outlets, switches, and plugs there are, but I do want to know whether they are charging $400 or $800 to replace those items. Line-by-line comparisons may enable you to actually help the contractor get better materials or cut down on material costs, particularly if some items are too high-end for the project. If normal doorknobs work on your project and they only cost $8 per piece, but the contractor budgeted in doorknobs at $34 per piece, help the contractor cut the costs and win the bid. You do have to realize that on a line-by-line bid a contractor will make some money on some items, nothing on others, and a lot of money on a few. Don't beat them up too much on single lines, as that might be all of their profit for the entire project. If the final number works and the contractor and you jibe, give him or her a try.

Once you have decided on the contractor you are going to use on your project, find out when work can start. Ideally, it can start the day after you close on the property. Most licensed general contractors will have some sort of contract or agreement stating you will pay them x number of dollars for x amount of work. You want to make sure that this agreement states:

1. The contractor is liable for anyone they bring on to the project whether it be an employee, subcontractor, or some other person.

2. The contractor is responsible for paying all subcontractors and for resolving any subcontractor grievances.

3. The contractor is insured.

4. The start date and payment draws, which include the work that is supposed to be done and when.

5. The estimated completion date.

6. All additional work not included in the contract, any change orders, need to be in writing and be signed by the owner of the property (this means the contractor can't do a bunch of additional work and charge you for it if you never approved it).

Change orders should *always* be in writing. A change order is a change to the original bid, which can either lower or raise the bid. Typically, they will go up and not down. There are some contractors who live off change orders. They purposefully bid the project low at the beginning and know that they will be adding more throughout the course of the project. They know that once they have their foot in the door with you, you are most likely going to see the project through with them. This is another reason to get those three bids; if you are comparing bids by line item, you can make sure they are not omitting anything. Beware the change orders and make sure they give you proof! For small items I will ask the contractor to send me pictures or I will video call with them to see what the problem is. For larger items I, or my boots on the ground, will do an on-site inspection. Most importantly, change orders and their costs need to be approved *before* the work is completed. I had one project in Florida where the contractor tried to include about $5,000 worth of electrical and drywall work on the final bid that was never approved. He had no pictures and never mentioned it to me during the 2-month project, and we had a contract that clearly stated any additional change orders had to be in writing and approved by me. When I asked him what the additional charges were for, he described what they were and what he did and why he did it. None of the additional electrical work was necessary, and it created additional drywall work that needed to be done. I told him I wasn't going to pay him the $5,000, as it was unnecessary and did not follow the rules of our contract. He threatened to put a contractor's lien on my property and said he would just get the money when I sold. When I asked if he wanted to get the lawyers involved, he quickly backed down. I still gave him $1,000 of the $5,000, as there was some added value to what he did, but not to the extent that he tried to swindle me. Beware of change orders and always get proof.

Not all contractors will be formal with their agreements; some will just send you an email, some will write them on a napkin, and some will have a twenty-page contract. You just want to make sure that there is an understanding and you have something in writing stating what each side is agreeing to, even if you have to write it out yourself. A lot of contractors may ask for 25–50% of the project upfront. If it is a new contractor, I might give them around 10% of the project ($2,000–5,000) to get started. This will pay for the initial demolition, dumpster, and labor costs. A good contractor will have enough money or credit to buy materials out of his or her own pocket to keep the project going. You do not want to write a check for $20,000 so the contractor can buy the materials and then have the contractor skip town! I do not give a contractor any money until the actual start day. I have heard stories of investors giving their contractors 50% of a project upfront and a month before the contractor even is going to start. This is crazy; don't do it; it is too risky. Additionally, the payments should make sense within the time frame of the project. A $20,000 remodel project shouldn't take 3 months; likewise, you shouldn't expect a $100,000 remodel to be done in 3 weeks. On average, for every $5,000 to $10,000 on a quote, expect 1 week of time. For example, a bid of $30,000 should take around 3–4 weeks to be completed.

If your contractor came from an ad you posted and not from a referral, be sure to ask for references. The typical reference will be a friend, family member, or even one of their subcontractors, not a past client. You can also check their company out online for reviews on Yelp, Facebook, and other websites. I personally prefer to see their actual work before I hire them. I ask them to walk me through a current project they are doing. If they don't have a project, I tell them to let me know when they do. If their hiring is contingent on viewing their work, they will typically get you in. Is the work site clean, does the work look good? If it was for a homeowner, get the homeowner's contact information and ask him or her for a review.

Check before you check. Remember this. When your contractor is asking you for another check, you must check the progress on the project. If it is minimal or no work has been done since your last payout, why is another check needed? Additionally, you should make your payment process systematic. You don't want a contractor showing up at your door demanding a check right then and there. I tell all my contractors that check requests must be made on Wednesday and I will give the checks on Friday. This allows me enough time to review progress on the project before I put another check into a contractor's hands.

You need to have contractors and handymen on your team. Every state is different with respect to general contractor licensing. In some states you only need to pay an application fee, while other states require extensive education, bonding, and insurance. No matter what the rules are, you have to trust your gut. If you think something is off, move on. There are going to be more contractors who want to work with you. You just have to put in the time to find them. Some jobs will require permits, and the contractor should have a knowledge of what is needed or not needed and be able to handle all of this. Remind the contractor that the property will be a flip, which means the buyer will be getting a home inspection and anything that doesn't pass will have to be fixed. This is a way of making sure the contractor does the work correctly the first time. Hire professionals when it is needed. A big job should be done by a professional company, someone who is responsible, has insurance, and is accountable to a state contractors board. If you just go with a handyman on a job where a contractor is required, the job may be cheaper upfront, but in the long run it will typically cost you more money. Do your projects right, do them safely.

CHAPTER 7 FLIP TIPS

1. Don't lift a hammer, let the professionals do it.

2. Contractors are everywhere, never stop looking for them.

3. Request ten bids to get three.

4. Hold your contractor accountable.

5. The cheapest isn't always the best.

6. Review their work *before* you hire them.

7. Beware the change orders.

8. Check before check.

9. The right professional for the right job.

CHAPTER 8 –

The Gift—Selling Your Flip and
Collecting Your Profit

Your rehab is completed, and it's time to sell your house. Do you just hand the keys to your realtor and say, "Here you go, do your job"? No. First thing you need to do is decide who is going to list the home for you. You don't have to list it with the realtor you used to buy the house! I always tell my students a listing for a realtor is like a gift, but many realtors don't treat it like that. The reason why it is a gift is realtors use it for marketing, for lead generation, for prestige. They put a sign up in the front yard and they are telling the world "I'm so trustworthy and good at my job, people work with me and you should too!." A listing is a gift, and in this case, this gift needs to be earned. Find out what these realtors are going to do for this gift. What type of marketing are they going to be doing? They should be putting the property on social media, Craigslist, the MLS, and open houses for other realtors. Some realtors will do mailers to the neighborhoods, pre-MLS private tours, virtual tours, aerial drone tours, and more! There are many different ways to market a property. However, many, and I mean many, realtors just put it in the MLS and wait. You will get most of your buyers this way, but your realtor should be doing more so you can reach all potential buyers faster! A realtor will typically tell you "I'm going to put the property on the MLS and another forty websites!" Guess what? Those other forty websites pull the data straight from the MLS, and your agent isn't doing anything extra! Find out what the agent really is doing. This might be a time to negotiate commission too! Your listing agent will typically expect 3% for listing the property, and then you typically pay another 3% to the agent who brings you a buyer. That is 6% to realtors when you sell the property. Make them earn it. Most of my realtors don't get 3%. Why? Because I give them multiple listings, and they appreciate the gift of a listing, because it may lead to them getting other listings or other buyers as clients. However, some realtors are truly worth 3%. Those realtors are expert negotiators and problem solvers and get things done.

If a realtor can get you a price of $280,000 instead of $265,000, don't you think he or she is worth that full 3%? I do. Additionally, a realtor with a full marketing campaign that includes both online and off-line media as well as professional photos may be worth that full 3% too. Therefore, it is important to ask what the realtor is going to do for you. Notice, we haven't even touched upon list price in this conversation. Some people go to a realtor who says, "I can list your house at $300,000," but if the house is really only worth $270,000, listing at $300,000 will prolong your marketing time, and once a property sits on market, potential buyers may suspect it has problems. After you drop your price a few times, they see you as a motivated seller, and that's when the lowball offers come in. A house that could have sold at $270,000 may now only get offers at $240,000–250,000! List price matters, but don't pick your listing realtor because he or she gives you the highest list price. Pick a realtor who has a solid marketing plan, is a good communicator and a good negotiator, and cares about your bottom line as well! A listing is a gift.

You need to get multiple opinions on the list price. The market will have changed over the several months it took you to buy the house and rehab it. Check your comparables again! By this time, you should have already established yourself with a few realtors and can call on them to give you a list price for your property. I will typically just send realtors a Dropbox.com link to a folder of photos of the property so they can get a good idea of what it looks like. Some will ask to walk the property, that's fine, but realtors are trained to get a foot in the door and a listing contract into your hands. Don't bow to the pressure. Let them know upfront you may not list with them, but you would appreciate their help and expertise on determining a list price. One of two things will happen. They will give you a list price and data to back it up *or* they will say they will only do it if they get the listing. If they are too busy to do you a favor (and possibly make money) they are not realtors you want to work with. Better to find that out now rather than later. Just as before, I want the same data set for my comparables; however, this time, I want to know what my competition is. That means active listings, pendings, and contingents. If all the sales are at $300,000, but there are seven similar listings at $250,000–260,000, I am not listing at $300,000! You will probably be the last house to sell if you do that, or you will never sell at all. A really good realtor may even walk some of your competition to see what they have or don't have compared with your property. The main thing with list prices is to make sure you are not overpriced.

When determining your list price, it is important to understand your market and how it reacts to list prices. There are some markets in which houses rarely sell above list price. In these markets, you would want to list your property slightly above where you want to sell it. If you think you will get a sale price of $290,000, you may want to list your property at $299,000. Why not $305,000? Because buyers looking for a house typically search within their budgets and in $25,000 increments. You may lose potential buyers who can only afford $300,000 if you list at $305,000. In other markets, it is common to list at a starting point, almost like auction bidding. I have seen houses listed at $520,000 that sold at $585,000. Your realtors will be able to not only tell you but show you the market trends. Your comparables are a good place to look to see a snapshot of this trend, did they sell above or below their asking prices?

The main thing is that you pick the realtor you think is going to do the best job, not the cheapest and not the one who necessarily gave you the highest list price. Someone who answers his or her phone and email, someone who sounds friendly, and someone who knows the difference between a good offer and a bad offer. Things that I have my realtors always do:

1. Professional pictures: No matter how good the agent thinks he or she is, a professional photographer is always going to be better. Always put a minimum of fifteen pictures in your listings. A typical professional photographer for real estate listings should run $100–200, and you can find them on Craigslist, Yelp, Facebook, and other websites. If you really liked the pictures of one of the comparables, have your agent get that photographer! If you are paying your agent a full 3%, he or she should be paying for the photographer.

2. Electronic lockboxes: I always have my agents put electronic lockboxes on my properties. An electronic lockbox will be able to track your showings down to the date, time, and agent who viewed your house. Many of these systems have automatic feedback emails that can be sent to the buyer's agents, so you can get feedback on your property. Whether they liked it, what they thought of the price, and so on. This is a typical feature in large market areas. If your MLS does not have this, your market may be smaller than recommended. I have my agents send me all of the email notifications they receive when there is a viewing; this way I know firsthand whether my properties are being viewed and how often. NOTE: I still leave my mechanical lockbox on the property so that I (or my boots on the ground or contractor) can access the property without the hassle of having my realtor let me in. This is also good if you ever need to make repairs, maintain landscape, adjust thermostats, and so on.

3. Open houses: I typically don't allow open houses at my properties. It is a way for agents to find new clients; you don't often sell a house at an open house. If your realtor is

going to hold an open house, I recommend that he or she does it prior to the listing going on the MLS and that he or she advertises the week before to other realtors, as they are more likely to bring in a real buyer. Ninety percent of the people who come to a regular open house are just the neighbors coming in to have a look. Do you really want a bunch of people tramping through your home, dirtying up your new flooring, and using your toilets? I never let other agents hold an open house at my properties. If your property looks good, you will get asked. It's just more wear and tear. If anyone holds an open house at your property, it should be your realtor.

4.   Sign in the yard: As soon the exterior of my property is completed, I allow my realtor to place a sign in the front yard with a rider (a smaller sign attached to the top or bottom) stating "coming soon" or "new listing." This way they have a chance of actually bringing in the buyer themselves, and the deal is easier to control. It doesn't always happen, but when it does, it is a nice little bonus for everyone.

5.   Marketing: My realtors will typically place our properties on their Facebook pages and Craigslist and will even create a private Web page just for the property. In our online world there are so many ways for a realtor to market the property, so they better know what their options are. I love it when my realtors tell me they are going to try something new!

6.   Listing comments: Once my property is listed in the MLS, I have my agent send me a copy of the agent full report, the MLS printout that the other agents see. I want to make sure that everything is accurate and as sexy as can be. Use verbs and adjectives in your descriptions of your property, don't just state the facts. Would you be excited about buying a: "Four-bedroom, two-bathroom house with 1,722 square feet and an attached garage. The back yard is fenced. Property has had recent remodeling." Or would you want to buy a "Newly remodeled home with all the bells and whistles. New Shaker cabinets and granite slab countertops in the chef's kitchen, vaulted ceilings throughout the living areas, and a separate master bed and bathroom with walk-in closets! The backyard is an entertainer's dream with mature landscaping and a fire pit for s'mores in the evening! Nothing else like it!". Describe your buyer's dream, give it some pizzazz! There will be some restrictions on wording that MLS places on realtors, but as long as the description is fair, honest, and doesn't discriminate against anyone, you should be fine. Ideally, your agent has this flair, but don't be afraid to throw in your two cents.

7. Offers: I do *not* want my realtors telling me "they said they are going to send an offer" or "there is an offer on the way." More often than not, the offer they thought was coming over never comes, and I am stuck checking my email waiting for it, over and over again. Don't get my hopes up. If an offer comes over, then and only then, do I want to know about it. I ask for my realtors to forward the email that the other agent sent. Don't just save the attached offer to their computer and then send it to you in a separate email. What's the point of that? Send me all of it. Your realtor shouldn't hide anything from you. If you aren't an expert at reading contracts, have your agent help you with it; it's what they are getting paid to do. However,

make sure you remind your realtor not to forward your responses to the other side of a transaction; the conversations between you and your realtor should be kept private.

Some realtors will recommend that you "stage" your property. When your realtors are giving you the data on your list price, take a look at the comparables and see whether they were staged. "Staging" means the properties were furnished to look like they are being lived in when they are actually vacant. This gives potential buyers an idea of how a room can be laid out. An empty room can sometimes look very small, and placing a bed or a dining table in it can help show the true dimensions. There are professional companies out there who can do this, but check their work first. If you have a modern designed property with lots of grays, whites, and blacks, you want the furnishings to match. A good staging company will have multiple examples and lots of pictures to show you. You don't want to have to do the design work yourself if you are paying someone else to do it. An additional reason to stage a house may be due to large rooms that could serve multiple purposes. Many people cannot figure out where to put a table, a couch, and a rug in a large open-concept area. Staging can fix that problem and make a potential buyer into an actual buyer. A few rules of thumb on staging:

1. Keep the furniture smaller than the room—that is, a queen bed instead of a king, low-backed instead of high-backed chairs, and so on.

2. Minimal items on the walls. When buyers see mirrors, paintings, and pictures on the walls, they see nail holes and clean-up needed.

3. Do not clutter. Same staging companies design to their own tastes, and some have horrible taste! I've seen pictures where companies put so many fake plants in a house that it looked like a plastic jungle!

4. Make sure everything in the house can be sold! A good staging company is willing to sell their pieces to buyers. You can sometimes use these items as negotiating points.

5. Consider fake versus real. There are companies that specialize in fake items such as televisions and computers. Would you rather have a box that looks like a real television in a house or a real television worth thousands of dollars that could go missing? Go for the box in lower- and mid-level houses. Higher-end houses should have the real thing.

6. Virtual staging. A growing trend in staging is just doing it virtually. There are computer graphics companies that can make it appear your house has tables, beds, artwork, and more for a few hundred dollars! I've seen virtually staged houses with pool tables and work-out equipment! For upper-end properties, it's possible to even do a full virtual-reality walkthrough on your houses so your potential buyers can experience walking through the home without ever even setting foot in it.

7. Furnishings should complement the house. If something feels out of place to you, have them remove it. You or your boots on the ground should walk the property before letting potential buyers in. If a staging company blocked a walking area, it could turn off buyers from your home!

Throughout this whole process, from finding contractors, houses, realtors, money, and so on, you, as the real estate investor, have to make sure you keep your end goal in mind. Your goal when you are flipping a house is to sell and to sell quickly. As we talked about in chapter 6, investors love their AROI. If you can complete a project in 4 months start to finish, from your initial purchase to when you actually close on the sale, and you made $21,500 instead of your initial estimate of $24,050, the investor might be okay with it but not thrilled. However, if you tell them you made them an AROI of 45.5% instead of 23% they should be thrilled. When you can make your projects happen faster, your AROI should go up and everybody wins. Remember: under promise, overdeliver.

Sometimes projects go long, markets shift, estimates were inaccurate. Things can go wrong, there is risk in this business. Your goal should be to sell this house. If the market starts declining, lower your list price to the bottom of the pricing range. Get out while you can. A small loss is better than a big loss. If the market is stable or increasing, and you are not getting offers or showings, you will need to lower your price. If I am getting showings but no offers, I will typically lower my price $100.00 at the 2-week mark. The fact you are having showings lets you know your property is priced within the correct range, you just haven't had the right buyer walk it yet. The price drop will refresh your listing in the MLS and get it back on the radar of potential buyers. If you are not getting any showings after 2 weeks, you are listed too high and you may need to review your comparables again and drop your price $5,000–10,000. If I still don't have an offer on my property after 4 weeks on the market, I will do another price drop. Remember, if you are getting showings, only do small incremental price drops. If you are not getting any showings, you are just listed too high and need to drop that price.

Sometimes flippers fall into the trap of turning flips into rental properties. This typically equates into a bigger loss than if you were to have just sold the property. If you are flipping a property, you are typically putting nicer finishes into it than you would if your original plan was to make it a rental. This is typically to the tune of 30% more spent on the rehab. As soon as you put a renter into a property, you've lost that 30% you spent. Your property is no longer newly remodeled. The carpet isn't new, the paint isn't new, it is a lived-in property. On average, across the country, a tenant-occupied property will sell for 8–15% less compared with a ready-to-move-in property. Additionally, tenant-occupied properties typically have longer marketing times, as most buyers are not looking for a tenant-occupied property, they are looking for a property they can move into. Instead of prolonging your losses, stick to your original plan and sell that house!

CHAPTER 8 FLIP TIPS

1. A listing is a gift to a realtor, find out how they are going to earn it.

2. Before listing, get three opinions of what your list price should be.

3. A good realtor is worth a full commission.

4. Reach all potential buyers as fast as you can.

5. Always have access to your property, stay in control.

6. If your comparables are being staged, yours should be too. Staging should match the design of the house.

7. Communication is key, don't just sit and wait for things to happen. Know what is happening.

8. Don't be passive with your listing. Reduce the price if the market is not accepting it.

9. Keep your end goal in mind. A house you bought to sell should be sold, not rented.

CHAPTER 9 –

Contracts and Closing—Maximize
Your Profit Potential

If you have done a good job on your remodel and you have priced your property correctly, you should be getting offers within your first 14 days on market. If no offers are coming in, have your agent double-check the listing in the MLS and send you a copy of the agent full report so you can see what the agent is saying in both the public and agent-to-agent remarks. Once the contracts start coming in, remember, just like when you send out a contract, the contracts on your property are the start of a conversation. You will have unrealistic buyers making offers on your properties. Prices will be low, they will bad mouth the workmanship, closing dates will be prolonged, etc. Don't take anything personally. More importantly try to find out the motivation of the buyer! A typical buyer and buyers agent are going to be focused on getting your property for the lowest price possible. It's just the way the game is played. Contract points that you should be aware of:

1. Purchase price: This one is pretty obvious, the higher the better. However, it's not always the most important number, because if you have multiple offers, they are probably

all near the same price; it will be the terms and conditions that have the potential to lower or increase your net profit.

2. Loan type and closing cost assistance: Cash offers are golden, but the majority of the houses you sell will be contingent on financing. The buyer will have to have a preapproval for a loan—either a conventional loan, a FHA loan, or a Veterans Affairs (VA) loan.

   a. Conventional is preferred, because this typically means the buyer is putting between 5 and 20% down and is a stronger buyer.

   b. FHA buyers are typically only putting 3% down and also will be asking you to pay for closing costs. Most entry-level buyers of remodeled properties purchase with FHA loans. If your sales price is more than twice what you paid for the property, the buyer will need two appraisals. Additionally, contracts with FHA financing can only be placed on a property after 90 days from the date you purchased it. These are just a couple of the items to be aware of when negotiating terms with an FHA buyer. FHA buyers typically will request 3% of the purchase price in closing costs, meaning if the purchase price is $220,000, they want $6,600 to go toward their loan, so their offer is actually only $213,400. A full-price offer does not always equate to a full price.

   c. VA buyers are people who have served in the military and will typically put a minimal deposit down as well; however, this should not be considered a weak offer. I generally give VA offers first shot at my homes. VA buyers also typically ask for assistance with closing costs. I don't flinch at their requests for closing costs, as it is just a little way I can give back to those that have done so much for us.

3. Earnest money deposit. The higher the EMD, the stronger the offer. Even on our low-end properties we ask for $5,000 EMD. Offers typically come in with only $1,000 to $2,500 in EMD; this becomes a negotiating item for you. You can raise the purchase price but keep the lower EMD as a trade-off. It doesn't cost you anything but looks like a give and take in the negotiating process, and you are the winner!

4. Financing company: I always look at the buyer's preapproval and want to make sure it is a good local company. If the property is in Atlanta but the mortgage provider is in San Antonio, I am going to question their ability to close. Additionally, I rarely sell to buyers who get financing from the big banks. In my experience, these loans end up going longer than they need to and typically do not close. Most real estate investors prefer that their buyers get their loans from a local lender/broker because you can actually call the person making money on the loan for status updates.

5. Closing date: Most local lenders/brokers can close in 30 days if they are pressed. They typically will ask for 45 days so they can be a little lazy and not have to operate under the gun. Well, guess what? Every day you own that property you are giving up profit. If I have two offers and one can close in 30 days and the other is asking for 45+ days, you know I am taking the 30-day offer.

6. Contingent on closing another property: I rarely accept an offer when it is contingent on the closing of a property

owned by the buyer. This means they need to sell their house to free up the money to buy your house. What if that property doesn't close? You just wasted your time and therefore your money. The only time you should be willing to do this is if:

a.   Buyer's property has already been appraised at or above sales price.

b.   Due diligence has already been completed by the buyer of your buyer's property.

c.   You are provided with escrow and loan company information for the buyer of the buyer's property.

d.   Closing is imminent, typically within 14 days.

The one exception to these four rules is if the buyer of your property is willing to release their EMD after their due diligence period on your property. This means the EMD goes into your pocket before the buyer even closes on your house. Only serious buyers will agree to this. If they fail to buy, you get to keep the EMD and typically come out ahead, despite the loss of time and additional carrying costs.

7.   Due diligence time frame: Standard due diligence on a single-family home is 7–12 days. This gives the buyer enough time to get a home inspection and review the findings. Additionally, they should be able to get their appraisal back in this time frame as well. If a buyer is asking for 20 days, we tell them 10. Remember, it's all a conversation.

8.   Title/escrow company: If you have a title insurance binder policy, you want the buyer to use your title company. You

decide whether you are getting a title insurance binder policy when you purchase the house. This will allow you to get discounted rates on your title insurance by committing to sell the house with the same title/escrow company you bought it from. It's a way for the title/escrow company to ensure repeat business. This can typically save you about a half percent of your ARV ($1,000 for every $200,000). I have heard multiple times from buyers' agents that the buyer is insisting they use their title company because their brother-in-law works there, and they will get a discount. I tell them "Cool, we can use them, however, our price bumps from $220,000 to $222,000, as I have a binder policy and it will cost me more to use their title company." Well, guess what? The buyer doesn't really have a brother-in-law working there, it's the buyer's agent who is trying to steer them there, because they get a $50 or $100 kickback for everyone they send to their title company! Imagine the buyer's agent trying to convince the buyer of that? They will usually go with your title company.

9.   Money for repairs and inspections: We typically will not have a problem with a buyer asking us to cover $500–1,000 for repairs to the property. A home inspection will probably find multiple things wrong with the property. Mostly minor items like an outlet not working, a noisy bathroom fan, or loose cabinet doors. Items that your contractor will typically fix for free, because they were his or her responsibility from the start; however, these repairs can be added up to that $500 to $1,000 on paper. It's another one of those items that looks like you are giving in but really shouldn't cost you anything. As for inspections, we always make the buyer pay for any inspections they

want. Why? Because they are the ones who want them. This is standard practice. When buyers pay for inspections, appraisals, certifications, and so on, they become financially invested in a deal and are more likely to close. If you do agree to pay for an inspection, don't pay for it upfront—reimburse the buyer at the closing table. This way, if the buyer back out, it's their loss, not yours. If your buyer does ask for repairs, make sure they don't just send you the home inspection and say "Fix it all". Have them spell out specifically what they want fixed and how they want it fixed. This should all be done by the agents on an addendum to your contract.

If you do have multiple offers on your property, you can use what is called a multiple counteroffer form. It lets the buyers know you are negotiating with more than one potential buyer. Sometimes when I do this I have my realtor communicate with only one party at a time; that way, if the first one just flat out says no to my counteroffer, I have the other offer I can accept, instead of scaring away both potential buyers. A good agent will know these tricks and will be able to juggle multiple buyers. The buyer, just like you did, will have the due diligence time period to inspect the property to see whether everything looks good. Expect the buyer to find issues with your property and don't take it personally; they always do. A buyer will get a home inspection on the property during the due diligence time frame. The home inspector doesn't feel like he or she did a thorough job unless there are some red marks on the report. There really are two types of inspectors:

a. The "it's not a big deal" inspectors go through a house, do their job, mark their findings, and point them out to the buyer. Typically, they realize that an outlet not working or old water staining on a roof eave is not a big deal. You want this type of inspector. Everything can be fixed.

b. The "sky is falling" inspectors take a buyer by the hand and point out the outlet that is not working and say, "Well, the outlet isn't working. It could be as simple as it needing to be replaced; however, since I can't see inside the wall, it could also be that the electrical lines are all messed up and you will have to tear into the drywall and redrill two-by-fours and cut into the ceiling, and that's if the electric panel can handle it. You better get a fully licensed electrician to come in here and inspect the entire system and maybe even replace it." Do you think a buyer wants to deal with those kind of headaches? This type of inspector can kill a deal for you, but there is little you can do about it. The realtors should be able to handle some of these guys; that's why it's best if your realtor can be there for the actual inspection! Put the fire out when it starts.

The home inspector is chosen by the buyer, but by having your realtor or even your contractor there, you can typically catch a lot of these problems on the spot so they don't escalate into the sky is falling scenario. But be prepared—some home inspectors will be at a house for 3 or 4 hours!

If your buyer is getting a loan, he or she going to be required to get an appraisal. I will have my realtor meet the appraiser at the property to let them in and to also hand over, yes, physically hand the appraiser, an improvement list. This is a list of changes I made to the property to improve it. If you want, you can include a couple of pages of before and after photographs if the house was in really bad

shape. Attached to the improvement list, your realtor should provide the comparables used to determine your list price. This should
all be done nonchalantly by your realtor, as they acknowledge the
appraiser is the expert (get on their good side, sweet talk them). But
they are providing it "just in case." Again, a good realtor will know
how to handle this. Making it personal by handing the improvement
list to the appraiser is better than your realtor giving the appraiser
a lockbox code and emailing the paperwork. What happens if the
appraisal comes in low? Well, the buyer will typically think "Yeah
for us!" and assume you are going to lower the price to the appraised
value. If the purchase price is $220,000 and the appraiser only came
in at $212,000, that is $8,000 out of your pocket! Don't you think
that is worth fighting for? If the appraisal comes in low, your realtor
should do two things:

1.   Ask the buyer if they are coming in with the additional
      funds to close.

2.   If the buyer says no, your realtor should write a "rebut-
      tal" to the appraisal. This should reiterate what was done
      to the property, what errors may be in the appraisal, and
      what comparable sales the appraiser should have or could
      have used instead of the ones that were used.

If the appraised value still does not change, you have a few
options. The buyer is going to want the price to be the appraised
value, because he or she doesn't want to overpay and can only get
a loan based on the appraised value, not the contract price. If you
are giving the buyer any incentives or closing costs, you can renegotiate these as well. If you were giving the buyer $6,600 in closing
costs and maybe a home warranty and some repairs, cut those out.
You typically can meet at some middle ground that is favorable to

both parties. We prefer to reach a middle ground versus losing a deal and putting the property back on market. Remember, the longer you have a property, the more it costs you. Additionally, if that appraisal was an FHA appraisal, the appraised value is going to stay with the property for the next 6 months! Meaning any other FHA buyer is going to be at the same appraised value. Best to sell it now and move on to the next project if you can reach that middle ground. Remember, it's all a conversation.

So you've gotten through the due diligence time frame and appraisal, hopefully unscathed. The buyer is ready to close, and it's time for you to sign. I always ask for the final numbers and paperwork to be emailed to me before I go to the title/escrow office so I can read everything first and make sure it is right. Loan payoffs to my hard money or private lenders, closing costs and realtor commissions, fees to title, and so on. Everything should make sense. If you have any questions on anything, make sure you ask! I know a lot of people like to get a check from the title company when they close a deal. They take a picture and post it on Facebook and Instagram. It gives validity to what they say they were doing and proves any naysayers wrong. Just take note, your bank might not make those funds available for 7–10 days. I always have my title companies wire the funds to my accounts so the money is ready to go into my next deals as soon as possible. If you do get a check and want to post it on social media, make sure to cover up the:

1. Checking account number

2. Checking account name

3. Check number

4. Signature line

Whenever I posted a check in the past, I zoomed into the amount and the date so I didn't have to worry about blocking out anything. Let people know of your success, because investors want to work with other successful investors. Realtors and wholesalers want to work with people who are actually doing business. Congratulations, and I want you to let me know when you get these checks (or wires)! I love hearing success stories from other real estate investors.

CHAPTER 9 FLIP TIPS

1. Just like before, a buyer's contract on your property is the start of a conversation.

2. A full-price offer does not always equate to a full price. Know the costs associated with the offer.

3. Review your buyer's preapproval; you can approve or disapprove of the mortgage company.

4. The realtor should meet the appraiser at the property with an improvement report and comparables to ensure your value.

5. Negotiating on the middle ground is typically better than starting over with a new buyer.

6. Multiple buyers can be negotiated individually. Don't scare everyone away.

7. Your realtor should be there for the home inspection to keep the sky from falling.

8. Once it's sold, share your success. People want to work with successful people.

CHAPTER 10 –

Remote Investing—The Five Must-
Haves for the Remote Investor

My first flips were all in my own backyard. Properties I
could drive to and check on the contractors' progress, ones for which
I could meet face to face with my realtors. I could walk the property
whenever I wanted. As my business expanded, so did the locations
of my flips, and I soon realized that flipping houses remotely was a
whole different beast. Every market has its own special characteris-
tics and nuances. Some markets you have to use an attorney to close
the transaction, while others you use a title or escrow company. Some
markets you have to pay a small upfront fee to be able to have a due
diligence period. Some markets the contractors are put through a
rigorous education and testing course before they are given a license,
while in other markets they just have to fill out an application and
pay a fee. Some markets the realtor, not the seller or the buyer, gets
first dibs on the EMD if the deal falls out. Every market is different,
but that doesn't mean you should stay away or that you can't flip
houses there. You just need someone who knows that market inside
and out and can communicate with the people you need to deal with.
You need a trustworthy and solid pair of boots on the ground. For

remote investing, your boots on the ground is going to be your eyes and ears, your representative, and he or she is the most important part of being able to be successful when investing remotely.

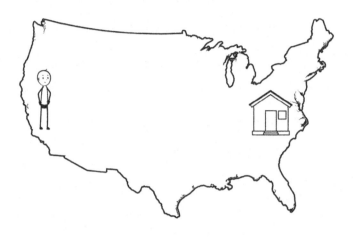

Your boots on the ground needs to be someone who is ambitious, wants to learn from you, and wants to make money with you. So do you just call up the boots on the ground store and order a pair? Wouldn't that be nice. In 2013 I began investing in Florida. I called and emailed realtor after realtor until I finally found a few who seemed to understand what I wanted to do and were onboard to make it happen. I began researching market areas, making offers, getting contractors, the whole shebang. At first, every deal these realtors and wholesalers brought to me were "amazing deals" and I "couldn't go wrong." Of course, they are going to say that! They want you to buy so they can make money. Remember, they get paid when you buy and sell properties, whether you profit on them or not. The properties that seemed to have the most potential, I'd make my offers, and if they were accepted, I would send my realtor out to begin my due diligence for me. I wanted the realtor to take my pictures and walk a contractor through the property. But the realtors didn't have the same sense of urgency I had. It was my money on the line, my EMD sitting at the seller's broker's office. I would get the pictures of the property from the realtor a day or two after the walkthrough, and there would be pictures missing, maybe the realtor forgot to take pictures of some of the major items. It's nice to know whether your flip needs an HVAC system or a new roof at $8,000 apiece. The realtor was too busy talking with the seller, the contractor, the listing agent. I would sometimes get the bid back from the contractor noting the property needed hazardous mold removal or a new staircase, but I had no pictures of these damaged areas. I'm not saying a realtor can't be your boots on the ground, but sometimes it's best to not give people too many hats to wear.

The same goes for contractors. I have heard from other investors who use contractors as their boots on the ground. They trust the contractor; the contractor does great remodels and really knows what to look for. But just like the realtor, the contractor is going to make money on the project regardless of whether you do. Contractors love to spend your money, and they will replace anything, even if it isn't broken or could just be fixed. What's that? You have a contractor who said he or she is going to do the project at cost? Awesome, good for you ... but that's not going to happen. "At cost" should mean the contractor is only charging you for material and labor. Guess what? The contractor is making money on both materials and labor but just didn't give you a line item on the bid for overhead or profit. I've had a lot of contractors all over the country present deals to me. They tell me it's a great deal. They will manage the project and do it at cost. They know the realtor who is selling the property and who can also list it for me when it's completed. Wow, sounds like a slam dunk. And all I have to do is provide all of the funding? Wait, they also have a hard money lender ready to go on the property, so all I have to do is provide the gap—the difference and the carrying costs? Now I only have to provide a small amount of funds, the contractor and I will split the profits 50/50, and I can just sit back and watch the magic happen. Stop right there! Who makes money on this deal? The realtor makes 6% upfront, because he or she is the listing agent and represents you on the purchase. The contractor does, because even though he or she says the job is being done at cost, they are getting a little something back from everyone else involved in the deal, referral fees. The hard money lender makes money off the points and interest. Where do you make your money? You only make money if the property sells for a profit. With so many hands in the cookie jar, you will be lucky to get a crumb. My question to people who present me these deals—whether it be the contractor, the realtor, or the money guy—is always: "If it's such a slam dunk, why don't you just do the deal yourself?" You will never get an answer from them that you will feel good about. Don't fall for these deals, don't risk your money this way.

If you can't trust realtors and contractors to be your boots on the ground, who can you trust? In Florida, after I hit a few of these hurdles and put too much trust in the wrong people, I searched my network. I found other investors who wanted to be in this business but were struggling for one reason or another. But I could see they were actively trying and had good attitudes. Someone who maybe hadn't done a deal yet or had a only a few deals going on. They are local to the market, they know how to talk and deal with the people, and they can operate as my representative. My *impartial* boots on the ground. But why would somebody I don't know or only know from Facebook be willing to do this? What does that person get out of it? The primary driver for these individuals will be experience. Remember how I have said people want to work with other people who have had success? If these boots on the ground can help you find, manage, and flip a property, they can now use that as their experience as well. Additionally, I recommend giving these individuals some sort of profit share. Depending on the amount of work you are having them do and what their experience is, 5–10% of the net profit is not unreasonable. If the project stands to net $40,000, don't you think it is worth it to pay someone 5% to help you see the project through to the end? That's only $2,000 to not only solve headaches when they happen but to keep them from happening. Good boots on the ground can help you from overpaying the contractor on change orders, can make sure the property is being properly maintained, and can just give you that peace of mind. There are plenty of people who will be your boots on the ground and not ask for a dime; they just want to learn. If I am wanting to deal in Boise, Idaho, I'll go onto Facebook and look up real estate–investing groups in Boise and also place an ad on Craigslist stating exactly what I want.

> I need boots on the ground to help me flip houses. I have several properties in the works and I want someone to be my eyes and ears. You must be able to take pictures, visit the property when needed, talk to contractors, and just be a helper. In return, you'll get the experience of actually flipping a house from start to finish and get a hands-on education. You must be reliable and have

reliable transportation. This may take an hour or two a week and the project will take about 4–5 months.

Free education will get you replies, but interview them and see what their current real estate story is. It has to be someone you feel good about and someone who is close to the property. If someone lives an hour away, he or she isn't the right person. You need someone who wants to learn, and even though you may be new to the business yourself, you do have plenty of knowledge that can help them be successful with you.

Remote investing is not just about having a solid pair of boots on the ground, you also need trust. Trust in the people you are working with, even though you are having them double-checked; trust in the numbers of your deal; and trust in yourself. If you can't trust people, you shouldn't do remote investing—it's as simple as that. When I first started investing remotely, I had trouble trusting people, but I did trust in myself, and I did trust in my system and my numbers. The people could be trained.

You do have to understand that people will take some leeway with your trust. They may tell you something is going to get done on Monday, but it's not done until Wednesday. Even though you trust people, you still have to hold them accountable, and that is where your boots on the ground come in. If someone knows you or your boots on the ground will be checking up, they will be more likely to do what was promised and in a timely way. A contractor is more likely to complete the project on time. A realtor is more likely to get a lockbox on a property. A landscaper is more likely to mow the yard. Trust, although given, still needs to be earned. Let your team know you have someone looking over their shoulders.

Your boots on the ground is your local representative, and you need to be able to communicate clearly with them. Have you ever had someone try to describe something to you over the phone, and you had no idea what that person was talking about? In our technological world, we can get past all of these hurdles. There are so many different ways to communicate now. Programs like Skype and FaceTime will allow you to actually walk a house with your boots on the ground. You don't want to be staring at them during this process; they should be showing you the property. I like to have my boots on the ground go through a house first and get all of the pictures taken. They can look for any issues they see right from the start. Once they have done their first walkthrough, I then have them get me on the phone and they walk me through the house. I have them start at the front yard, just as though I got out of my car and was there myself. I do a full turn and look at all of the neighboring properties, and then I look back at my property.

Is my property conforming, does it fit in with the rest of the properties I see? If all of the houses you see up and down the street are one-story ranch houses and your property is a three-story, remember, you want to be an apple surrounded by apples. I then have them walk me through the house, showing me every room, looking in every closet, looking under every sink. I ask what they smell. Does the house smell bad or moldy? I want them to show me any problem areas. Depending on the size of the house, this process should take between 10 and 20 minutes. You get to actually walk the house, no matter how many hundreds or thousands of miles you are away. Trust but train. If you don't let people know what you need, want, and expect, they can't give it to you.

I've said it multiple times, and I will say it again, real estate investing has risks, and those risks grow when you invest remotely. You may have found a great team of people in a market area, you trust them, but you have also been training them along the way. What if something happens? What if there is a problem and nobody has a solution. What if your people stop answering their phones? Something will happen at some point in your remote real estate-investing career, and you will have to make decisions that will affect the outcome of that property. There could be tens of thousands of dollars in the balance on these decisions. If you are investing remotely, you must be able to go to the property if you are needed. This isn't to let an inspector in or to check to make sure the contractor painted the house the right color. This is for when there is a problem and you are the only one who can solve it. I had this happen to me on one of my first Florida properties, before I had a solid pair of boots on the ground. The house looked great, the remodel was done, the contractor had been paid, and the property was on market and getting showings. And getting showings. And getting more showings. But no offers. I asked the realtor what was wrong with the property. We were priced right; since we were getting showings, it had to be something wrong with the property. The realtor was telling me to just drop the price $10,000–15,000 and she knew she would be able to sell it at that price, but I knew the price wasn't the issue. I jumped on a plane and flew 2,300 miles to fix a problem. If you are investing remotely you have to be able to do this when the time comes: drop what you are doing, go to the property, and fix the problem. I spent about $1,500 on a plane ticket, hotel, and rental car, and I was in Florida for less than 2 days. I got there, went to the property with the realtor, and walked it with her in person. I opened up every cabinet, every door. I walked every room just like a buyer would have, and I found little issue after little issue. There was no shelving in any of the closets! It's a minor thing, but it tells potential buyers that this house is not complete and there are probably other things not complete. I walked into the kitchen and the first thing I noticed was there was no microwave above the stove, not even a hood vent. There was just a blank space. I asked the realtor if it had been stolen; she told me there never had been one. I went through my pictures of the property, and every picture that was sent to me was angled just the right way to not show that spot, even the professional pictures I had paid for. There were a number of other small things that were not done, were missing, or just added funk to the house that I couldn't tell from the pictures. I called the contractor up and asked why there wasn't shelving in any of the closets. He replied that some of it was broken, so he removed all of it. He had no answer when I asked why nothing was replaced. The microwave was on the bid but was never installed. In the end, I spent $1,500 for travel and another $700 on minor items. I took the property off the market for a week while the repairs were getting made. When the property went back on market (at the same price), I had an offer within 2 weeks at full list price. Could the realtor have sold it if I dropped the price $10,000–15,000, which was her fix? Sure she could have, but I would have been out $8,000 or more in potential profit. This was the reason why I started doing the video walkthroughs with my boots on the ground. On this house I had only received pictures from the realtor and had her walk the property with me on a voice call. In this business you are always learning and improving what you do.

Remote investing has more risk and with that should come more reward. I only do projects remotely if I have a larger profit line. I will raise my desired profit up 25%. So if I want to make a 20% ROI on a project in my home market, I will bump that up to 25% ROI in a remote market. Or for the calculation to determine my max offers, I go after 19% of ARV for profit instead of 15%. Invest smart, invest safely. The five things you need to invest remotely are:

1. Boots on the ground

2. Trust

3. Communication skills

4. The ability to go to the project when you are needed

5. More profit

As you grow in this business, you will see deals all over the country brought to you by all manner of people. People you know and trust and people who found you online. The deals may look good on paper, but without these five things, you will have greater risk.

CHAPTER 10 FLIP TIPS

1. Boots on the ground are key; you need someone willing to learn and work.

2. Trust and train. If you don't take the time to train people on what you need and want, you can't trust them to do it.

3. Look over everyone's shoulders and let them know you are doing it.

4. Get up and go when it is needed.

5. With greater risk should come greater reward.

CHAPTER 11 –

Beware the Black Hole—The
Power of Social Networking

When I first started out in this business, I was extremely solitary. If I was dragged to a party by my wife or one of my friends, I'd grab a drink and find a cozy place to sit, and I figured if someone wanted to talk to me, he or she would come find me. Well, guess what? That's not how the world works. If you want something, you must go get it. If you need something, you must tell people. If you want your life to change, you must change what you are doing.

I entered the world of social media in 2013, and the success my business enjoys today is a direct result of that decision. I am sure most of you reading this right now are already on some form of social media, whether it is Facebook, Twitter, Instagram, or LinkedIn. But are you doing it with *purpose*? Your time should be driven by purpose. Mine is. Before I pick up a phone to make a call, I decide what my purpose is, what my goal is for that phone call. If I don't determine my purpose before I get on that call, I could spend 15 minutes talking about pick-up trucks with a contractor. Not an efficient use of time. Before I go into the grocery store, I determine what my purpose is. Otherwise I walk out of the store with a box of donuts, sushi, and potato chips instead of milk, eggs, and flour. Knowing the purpose of what and why you are doing something is the key to reclaiming your time, and social media can be the number one destroyer of time management. How often do you go on Facebook to see what your friends are doing? How often do you scroll through pictures on Instagram? How often do you take a picture of food that you just ordered so you can let the masses know you are eating a baby spinach and quinoa salad with a cranberry-quince vinaigrette?

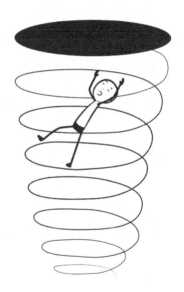

These activities become black holes: they distort your time and suck you in. You lose yourself in them. When I first jumped into social media, it was overwhelming how much information and how many people were out there. I began setting an alarm for 10 minutes, 15 minutes, or 30 minutes depending on what my activities were, what my purpose was. I would designate my purpose of entering the social media world and I would dive in and not let the distractions get me off course. My purposes varied. Ten minutes to post pictures or a video of a current project or a project in the works on a couple of groups for wholesalers. The purpose of this was not to just post pictures but to let these wholesalers know that I am really flipping homes and what markets I am investing in. A post with a picture or video typically gets more exposure and traction than just a text post. You want that picture or video to grab someone's attention as they are scrolling through their posts. Fifteen minutes to search out new groups of investors, wholesalers, and flippers and join them. Thirty minutes to create my profile on LinkedIn or Instagram with pictures and explanations about what I do and what I am looking for from others. You must let people know who you are and what you need. The "who you are" is not "Hi, my name is Luke. I grew up in Wisconsin. I am married to my beautiful wife and we have a hilarious son. I enjoy playing soccer and camping." Is your purpose in getting onto social media to let people know about your past? No! The purpose of getting onto social media is to build your future. My bios on social media typically read something along the lines of "Real estate entrepreneur who has flipped hundreds of houses across the country and has raised millions of dollars. I am looking to join forces with others who have money or houses or want to learn about this business." A good example for someone who is just starting out in this business could be: "Real estate flipper located in St. Louis, if you have a house you are selling or money you need to invest, contact me today." People will research you. People will look you up on social media and let that be a decider of whether they are going to work with you. You must have a presence on social media, but it must be related to what you are doing and what you need. When I got into social media, I made the decision it was going to be business-centric. I wasn't going to just put family and food pictures out there for the world to see. I was going to put fishing lines in the water and start catching some leads. Every day I receive new connections and friend requests from people I have never met or spoken with and who are located across the globe. I accept these friends and connections, as they typically found me from a post I put in a group somewhere, or we have a mutual connection between us, or they just did a random search on house flipping or real estate investing and found me. Your network can be your net worth. The more you network and find other people or give other people the ability to find you, the more your net worth can grow, as long as you are doing this with purpose.

You have to start networking with the right people to begin with. When you are first starting out, you need to be bigger than you are. Start sending out those friend requests to people who are actually working in this business. Right now I want you to go on to Facebook and find a real estate–investing group, either local to your chosen market or a national group; find five people who have photographs of houses they are rehabbing, properties they are demolishing, or properties that are fixed up and they are selling; and send them a friend request. Do you need to scroll through a year's worth of posts and pictures to find these people? No, there is typically a search bar for a group page, and you can just type in "St. Louis" or whatever market you are in. Surround yourself with people in this business. Always remember the purpose of why you are doing something. If you want someone to invest with you, remember, they will research you. If they go to your profile page and all they see are pictures of you with your twenty pet ferrets, they probably will think you are not a serious real estate investor. If they go to your Facebook page and see a picture of you holding a couple of tile samples at Home Depot with the caption "Looking for some material for my next project," that is credibility. You can do that picture today, even if you don't have a project in the works. I see a lot of people who post a picture of a beautiful kitchen or bathroom from a magazine or a hotel they stayed at and they caption it with "I wish I had this in my house." A better caption would be "Inspiration for my next flip." Remember, just like we talked about in developing your real estate story, the words you choose create people's perception of you. Post pictures of ugly houses you walked, even if you don't get them under contract; it shows people you are actively doing this business.

At this point I know some of you are thinking that you don't want your families to know you are taking this crazy leap into real estate and what if you don't become successful? What if you fail? What if there is no support? The fact is there are going to be people who will say you can't do this. People who you think love and care about you will laugh at you and say awful things that will destroy your drive and confidence. Sadly, this is the way our world works. But there are people out there who will support you. Some close to you will see your dreams and encourage them; others you will find along your journey. I made a very early decision in this business that if someone didn't support me and what I wanted to do, they were gone. There is no reason to surround yourself with negativity and ill will. You can succeed in this business. I have seen people who started with nothing become millionaires. I have had students with a couple thousand dollars in their bank accounts buy, fix, and flip multiple houses in their first year. It can happen, so why shouldn't it happen to you? I know walking away from the negative people is easier said than done, especially when it comes to family. If you find you have family members who are unsupportive, just don't talk to them about what you are doing. Talk about your kids or the weather instead. If they ask you how everything is going in your business, tell them it's going fine and then ask about them. It's a difficult thing to walk away from family, but if that person is holding you down and surrounding you with negativity, you need to move past that to change your life.

I want you to get out a piece of paper, right now, and write down the five people you spend the most time with, be they friends, family members, or coworkers. When you look at this list, you will almost always see a couple of people who are in a worse position financially than you and a couple people who are a little better off than you. You will be somewhere in the middle of this wealth association chart. The fact is that this list of five people will and should change over time. If you want to better your position in life and reach financial freedom, you will see that people drop off the bottom of the list and news names will be added at the top. You must surround yourself with people who are better than you, smarter than you, more knowledgeable than you, if you want to change your current situation. However, this shouldn't just be about becoming more successful, this journey you are on should also be about being happier, having less stress in your life. Look back at that list of five people and you will see a range of happiness in those people as well. The more you surround yourself with happy people, caring people, stress-free people, the more that affects you. I have met many very successful people who were very unhappy, even mean people. They never made it onto my list of five. Although I am sure I could have learned something from them, that was not the direction I knew I needed to go in my life. Who would purposefully choose to fill his or her life with negativity, greed, or hate? There is no need for that. There are many people in real estate who have a scarcity mentality. This means they think there is not enough for everyone and they have to get it or have it all before you do. As I discussed earlier, there will always be plenty of houses to rehab, to rent, to build; there is an abundance in this world and there is enough for everyone. Surround yourself with positive people, ignore the negative, and watch your time, your energy, and your finances grow.

Networking is not just done on social media. Remember how I said I used to be the guy at the party who sat in the back of the room waiting for people to come to me? That was my comfort zone, that was my cocoon. I had to get out of that. I had to walk around with my gaze forward and not on the ground. I made myself become more social. I shook hands with people, I said hello to people I didn't know just walking down the street. I smiled. There are little changes you can make in your own behavior to let people in. When I was sitting in the back of the room, people didn't come up to me because my behavior told them I didn't want them to. You must network in this business to be successful, because you need other people in this business. You need realtors to bring you deals, wholesalers to find you properties, contractors to rehab the houses, investors to fund your deals. If you can't look them in the eyes, smile, and shake hands, you will need to learn these skills. This can all be done virtually over apps like FaceTime and Skype if you are rehabbing remotely. If you don't give some type of personal touch, people most likely aren't going to be there to help your business grow. I challenge you to go to a real estate–investing club meeting in your local market a minimum of once per month. Search around and you will find them out there. Meetup.com is a great tool to find these groups; just do a search for "real estate investing" and see what comes up in your local area. Some of these clubs will be free or will have a small fee to cover the meeting room and refreshments. Some clubs will have amazing speakers there to share knowledge. Others will have traveling salespeople selling their newest trick. No matter what is going on at the meeting, there will be time for you to shake hands with other investors in your area. Your purpose at this meeting is to always meet five new people. Do not leave that meeting until you have had five conversations with five different people and have told them who you are and what you need in your real estate–investing business and, more importantly, have asked them who they are and what they need. Your business will succeed because of the people you know and the connections you make. Additionally, the best conversation someone has is when they get to talk about themselves. I have had conversations with people where I spoke at most 5% of the time and let them do 95% of the talking, and the next day I get emails or calls from them letting me know what a pleasure it was to meet me and talk with me. I have even had people send me deals or ask to invest with me the very next day because of this little trick. As beginning real estate investors you may have a tendency to run at the mouth and just spew out all the information you have been accumulating. Don't. The person you are speaking to will go running for the hills. You have scared them away. Instead, let the other person talk. Ask questions.

Where else can you network? Anywhere you are. I'm not a golfer, but I know plenty of investors who are and get deals done on the links. I personally prefer a sports bar. I have had more real estate–investing conversations at bars than anywhere else. But these conversations can be had at the gym, in line at a grocery store, at your child's school, anywhere. This doesn't mean you have to go out and press the subject to everyone with a pulse who is standing within 10 feet of you. If you can make eye contact and smile at a stranger, these conversations will happen. They start with small talk and can go anywhere. Let people talk, ask them questions, find common ground. You never know who is a realtor. You never know who has a contractor in their family. You never know who is afraid of the stock market and is looking for another place to invest. They are out there and you can find them!

CHAPTER 11 FLIP TIPS

1. Do things with purpose. Know what you are doing and what you want to accomplish.

2. Time your tasks. It doesn't take an hour to post a photo.

3. Your network can be your net worth, but you have to make that happen.

4. Connect with those active in this business and never stop learning.

5. Network locally and nationally. Deals and money can come from anywhere.

6. Get off the chair and shake some hands. They won't come to you.

CHAPTER 12 –

Conclusion—Keeping the Business Moving

Real estate investing is a business of continuity. You can never stop looking for properties, money, or contractors. If you are missing one of these, your business will come to a halt. You will make mistakes in this business. You will be off on your numbers. You will have a contractor run away with your money. But if you do what I explained in the preceding chapters, you will mitigate those risks and you can truly find success.

Everything starts with your real estate story and goes from there. Once you know who you are, you need to start finding realtors, wholesalers, contractors, and money sources. You don't look for these one at a time, you look for all of them at once. This business only happens if you do it. You hold the keys to your success. It will always be easier for you to do the things that you have to do. You have to go to work in the morning. You have to go grocery shopping. You have to rake the yard. If you don't do the things that I outlined here in this book, will your boss yell at you in the morning? Will the dinner table be empty when you get home? Will the leaves pile up on your yard? Will I come to your home and yell at you? No, none of these things will happen. You will continue your life as it is. It is always more difficult to do the items that don't have consequences. Things like contacting realtors to start sending you deals, picking a market to invest in, running numbers on properties, connecting with other investors. If you don't do these things, your life won't change. You will continue down the path you are on. However, if you put the time and energy into this business, if you decide to do the extra work instead of watching the game or taking a nap, your path will change. I believe that you can do this. I have seen people start with nothing and become real estate rock stars. However, it takes many nights of hard work to become an overnight success. When you get frustrated or hit a bump in the road, don't give up. Reach out to your network and ask for help—you don't have to do this alone! There are many people out there who want you to succeed. I want to see your story grow! In fact, "The Flipping Blueprint" group is on Facebook for you to not only share your stories, but to also use for networking and to reach out for help. There is a whole group out there that wants to see you succeed, now is the time to join it!

There is always going to be more to learn, that process never ends. Each one of these chapters could be a book unto itself. There are always going to be more scenarios than there is room in a book. Just remember there is always a solution to any scenario, and many times there are multiple solutions. The purpose of this book was to give you a blueprint so you can start achieving the results you want. Instead of a real estate–investing crash course that just provided a floor, walls, and ceilings, you now have your structure *and* doors and windows, cabinets and countertops, flooring and lights. Within this book are many of the missing pieces most other educations don't provide or try to provide at break-the-bank pricing. Use what you have read. Use this flipping blueprint to build your future. You hold the power of the future in your hands. You decide which path you want to go down. Follow through with what was taught here, and you too can reclaim your time and achieve financial freedom!